OLAVE, LADY BADEN-POWELL
AND HER DERBYSHIRE ROOTS

PORTRAIT OF OLAVE BADEN-POWELL BY MR H.H.J. BAIRD IN 1904

Reproduced by courtesy of Chesterfield Girl Guides Headquarters

OLAVE,
LADY BADEN-POWELL
AND HER DERBYSHIRE ROOTS

WITH AN FOREWORD BY HER GRANDSON
ROBIN BADEN CLAY

JILL ARMITAGE

COUNTRY BOOKS

Published by: Country Books
Courtyard Cottage, Little Longstone, Bakewell, Derbyshire DE45 1NN
Tel: 01629 640670
email: dickrichardson@country-books.co.uk
www.countrybooks.biz

ISBN 978-1-906789-51-0

British Library Cataloguing in Publication Data.
A catalogue record for this book is available from the British Library.

Printed and bound in England by 4edge Ltd, Hockley, Essex

DEDICATION

To Isabel and Emma,
and the next generation of Guiding

DERBYSHIRE
County Council
Improving life for local people

Councillor Andrew Lewer
Leader of the Council
County Hall
Matlock
Derbyshire
DE4 3AG

Tel (01629) 580000 ext. 36022
Direct Line (01629) 536022
Email: andrew.lewer@derbyshire.gov.uk

County Councillor for the Ashbourne
Electoral Division (Conservative)

Jill Armitage

Chesterfield
Derbyshire

8 February 2011

Dear Jill Armitage

Unveiling of a blue plaque in honour of Lady Baden-Powell

I am delighted to invite you to join us for the unveiling of one of the Derbyshire County Council blue plaques.

This scheme was launched last year to celebrate Derbyshire's cultural and historical heritage. We received many nominations and after short listing and a public vote the first six to be honoured were determined. They are Richard Arkwright junior, Lady Baden-Powell, Jedidiah Buxton, Arthur Lowe, Joseph Paxton and George Stephenson.

The unveiling of the plaque to honour Lady Baden-Powell will take place on **Tuesday 22nd February** at 2.30pm in Shentall Memorial Gardens, outside the Town Hall in Chesterfield. This is an appropriate date as each year on the 22nd February Girl Guides all over the world celebrate World Thinking Day and think about all the Girl Guides and Girl Scouts around the world.

By kind invitation of the Mayor of Chesterfield light refreshments will be available beforehand in the Town Hall from 1.30pm.

Following the unveiling you are invited to the headquarters of the Chesterfield Girl Guides for refreshments and entertainment. The headquarters is within easy walking distance of the unveiling site at the junction of St Margaret's Drive and Cross Street off Saltergate. A map giving the locations is enclosed along with the event schedule. Please note that daytime parking is very limited in the immediate vicinity of the headquarters.

Continued ......

www.derbyshire.gov.uk

INVESTOR IN PEOPLE

CONTENTS

FOREWORD

I feel very honoured to be invited to write a foreword for this book. Some years ago Jill wrote a charming little book describing my grandmother's early childhood, and I am very pleased to be associated in a small way with this new book from her hand.

The earlier book is *The Derbyshire Childhood of Olave, Lady Baden-Powell, G.B.E.*, for Olave, Lady Baden-Powell was my Granny. Her ashes now lie in the same grave as her husband, in Nyeri, Kenya, where I was born.

Granny, however, had started her long life by being born in Derbyshire, in 1889, but my first visit to this county was not until 1960 when, as an Assistant Scoutmaster, I camped at the Chatsworth Jubilee.

Granny and other VIPs, including Granny's younger daughter (my mother Betty), were invited to a buffet lunch at Chatsworth House. In her diary, my mother wrote that my first cousins Robert and Mike B-P were "neat and sensible and well-behaved". My mother decided not to pass on my invitation because she thought that, being under canvas, I would not be smart enough. I don't think the Duchess would have minded.

On that occasion Granny wrote, in her Jubilee letter – "There are those amongst us that can look back over the last fifty years of Guiding and many more of you will be able to look forward to the next fifty." I would never have guessed how quickly those fifty years would pass, until fifty years later I returned to Derbyshire for the unveiling of the Blue Plaque in her honour, on Thinking Day, the 122nd anniversary of her birth, in Derbyshire.

In 1973, in her book, *Window on my Heart* (p.258), Granny

described her recovery from an operation, and the many, many letters she had received, not just from grown-ups, but particularly from girls themselves,

> *"I felt that as long as I had the strength and had something to contribute, and as long as people wanted to see me, I had a duty to go to them and to give them encouragement. I have never had much patience with committees and sitting round a table discussing rules and red tape. I like to be out 'in the field' where I feel I can use my own peculiar gifts.*

The duties of World Chief Guide have never been defined. I once wrote:-

> *Roughly you are expected to work all day and all night, to be completely at everyone's beck and call, to have the wits and intelligence of a University professor, the pen of a ready writer, to toss off messages, articles, broadcasts and even books as easily and quickly as you would a meal, to travel hither and thither the whole year round doing Conferences, Rallies, Meetings, be 'at home' to those who wish to meet you there. Visit Camps all over the world and also at the same time be available at home for 'quiet talks when you have a free day' and so on!"*

She was the first World Chief Guide; there has not been another. They don't make them like that any more.

I had the good fortune to live with my Granny for a year while I was a student, and it was a remarkable eye-opener, to see at first hand what she called "my own peculiar gifts" in action.

The word "gifts" does not do her justice; for much of it was just plain hard work imposed by self-discipline and a sense of duty, and tempered with consideration for others.

Granny would always do her homework before an event, going through her address books checking whom she was going to meet, and reading her brief notes on each. And after each function, she was assiduous in writing a personal letter of encouragement and thanks to each person involved – often a dozen or more.

She used to tour abroad in the winter months, partly because her apartment was very expensive and difficult to heat. These tours were always meticulously planned, and again, she did her homework. And she wrote those thank-you letters. Usually, she would be travelling on to another town the next day, and her Rule was that the letters had to be written and sent before starting the next journey, so she was often up until two or three in the morning, as she described it, "paddling around on my typewriter."

Granny also had a prodigious memory for people she met, frequently remembering, years later in a totally different context, a person she had met once and only briefly.

> The Scout and Guide Movements are
> the greatest
> non-sectarian
> movements for peace
> that the world has ever known.

They were started by B-P, but are what they are today to no little extent thanks to my Granny and her "peculiar gifts" to inspire. But these were inculcated in her early childhood, in Derbyshire, and I am so pleased and grateful that Jill has re-visited and explored further into that aspect of Granny's background.

Robin Baden Clay
April 2011

INTRODUCTION

The name Baden-Powell will always be identified with the Scout and Guide Movement throughout the world. Scouting is an organization for boys started in 1907 by Lieutenant-General Sir Robert Stephenson Smyth Baden-Powell, K.C.B.,(shortened to B.P.) but the girls wanted to get in on the action and a sister movement called Guiding was established a few years later.

The formation of Guiding also coincided with the marriage of B.P. to Olave St Clair Soames on October 30th 1912. Olave was a young lady of genteel birth who devoted her life to promoting Guiding. She is known throughout the world but few realise that Olave is a Derbyshire girl. She was born at Stubbing Court, Wingerworth. Her father had interests in a brewery in Chesterfield, and when Olave was only eighteen months old, they moved the three miles to West House in Chesterfield. After five years, they moved to their third Derbyshire home, Renishaw Hall, Eckington.

After leaving Derbyshire, Olave lived in many parts of the country. She travelled extensively promoting Guiding but in recognition of her Derbyshire roots she allowed a wreath of olives to be woven into the Chesterfield Guide Standard.

Her portrait in oils painted by Nathaniel H.J. Baird in 1904 now hangs in the Chesterfield Guide Headquarters which she officially opened in May 1930. There is also a copy of her birth certificate on the wall. She had been present at many Guiding events throughout Derbyshire including the Jubilee Camp held at Chatsworth in June 1960 to celebrate 50 years of Guiding.

Olave Lady Baden Powell G.B.E. is loved throughout the world and to honour this great lady, a blue plaque has been unveiled on the site of what was her Chesterfield home.

It is a fitting tribute which also marks 100 years of Girlguiding, and as a mark of respect and admiration the day chosen to unveil the plaque was February 22nd 2011, Olave's birthday which rather surprisingly she shared with B.P. In the Girlguiding calendar this is a special day celebrated every year by Guides and Scouts throughout the world as Thinking Day in honour of the Founders of the Scout/Guide movement.

Jill Armitage
2011

ACKNOWLEDGEMENTS

The idea for the first book *The Derbyshire Childhood of Olave, Lady Baden-Powell GBE* published in 1994 was only possible thanks to the help and support received from the Hon. Mrs Betty Clay, Olave's daughter, and Lady Patience Baden Powell, wife of Lord Robert Baden-Powell, Olave's grandson. Sadly neither of these two ladies are now with us.

The Hon. Mrs Betty Clay died in 2004. Lady Patience Baden-Powell died on December 18th 2010.

I am indebted to Mr Robin Baden Clay for his help, support and encourgement, and to the ladies of Chesterfield Guide Headquarters for their assistance.

My gratitude goes to the people who contributed to the original work which has formed the basis for this book. *Olave Lady Baden Powell and Her Derbyshire Roots* builds on the story of Olave's formative years in Derbyshire. It gives an overview of her life with special emphasis on her Derbyshire Guiding connections.

I am especially indebted to Chesterfield Guide Head Quarters who kindly allowed me to copy Lady Baden Powell's birth certificate, the photographs of the official opening, the Chesterfield Guide Standard and Olave's portraits.

For sourcing and supplying the early photographs, my thanks go to Andrew Roger Kaye, Chris Goodlad, John Thacker, John Hirst, Chesterfield local studies and the London Girlguide Head Quarters.

THE SOAMES FAMILY COMES TO CHESTERFIELD

There must have been brew houses in Chesterfield throughout its history. In 1697 that intrepid explorer Celia Fiennes said the town had the best ale in the kingdom, accredited to the fine well water found deep below the town. There was certainly no shortage of places supplying it. According to Baghsaw's trade directory of 1846, there were forty six hotels, inns and taverns and by 1872, Francis White's directory shows a startling increase to sixty seven plus fifty four beer houses, the vast majority of which were crammed into the 300 hundred acre town. It's not surprising to find that to supply these hostelries, Chesterfield became the second largest brewing town in Derbyshire.

The first large scale enterprise was the Brampton Brewery whose records go back to 1839 and probably earlier because the origin is unknown. It was the ownership of this brewery that brought the Soames family to Chesterfield in 1877.

Brampton Brewery, then known as Parkin and Co. Brewers and Maltsters, was run by a partnership of Osbourne and Chater. Along with the factories and the potteries, the brewery was a cornerstone of the local community.

In 1877, the business consisted of a brewery, sited in a triangle of land between Chatsworth Road and Wheatbridge Road, Brampton, Chesterfield (now the site of a Matalan superstore) together with fifty three licensed houses within a fourteen mile radius.

The business was offered for sale by auction on May 23rd 1877 at

BRAMPTON WITH ITS BREWERY, POTTERIES AND FACTORIES WAS AN
INDUSTRIAL AREA, AS THIS PARORAMIC VIEW FROM THE TOP OF ROBINSON'S
TOWER SHOWS. THE EXTENSIVE SIDINGS IN THE LANCASHIRE, DERBYSHIRE
AND EAST COAST RAILWAY YARD CAN BE SEEN, PLUS THE MIDLAND'S BRANCH
LINE CURVING AWAY TO BRAMPTON, CROSSING THE RIVER HIPPER

the Angel Hotel, High Street, Chesterfield. Before the railway era, this was one of the few coaching and posting houses in the town with stabling for one hundred and sixty horses. Having a large banqueting hall and a newsroom, it was also the meeting place of the Freemasons and of town council members.

In that hall on that day in May 1877, bidding for the brewery was brisk and when the hammer fell, the final bid of £48,000 had been made by Mr Arthur Soames, a maltster from Newark. The total purchase price including plant and contents was £60,000 to £70,000. Mr Soames handed over his share to his son Harold, and a partnership was formed between Mr Harold Soames and Mr Charles Hames Chater. By July 1877, transactions were complete and the company resumed trading as C.H. Chater and Co.

Harold Soames was the younger son of an old gentry family from Lincolnshire, being brought up at Irnham Park, a post medieval house rebuilt after an extensive fire in 1887. It is still privately owned.

Harold was twenty five and had just completed his studies at Eton and Cambridge when he became involved with the brewery. He was ethereal minded, a poet and artist with a wide knowledge of art and literature. He was not a hard headed business man but he was ambitious, industrious and impatient for progress. Together Chater and Soames set about expanding the business and two years later in 1879, the new outlets had necessitated the enlargement of the brewery. It's quite amazing that the beers were always so popular when one considers that Chesterfield was known for the strength of its Methodist Movement which supported abstinance.

BRAMPTON BREWERY BUILDINGS c1880

When he became involved with the brewery, Harold Soames and his brother Frederick took up residency in the area. Chesterfield at that time was a small market town, but they opted to live outside the town, three miles away at Wingerworth, and a property known as Stubbing Court.

According to *The Derbyshire Country House* Volume I; Craven and Stanley, the Stubbing estate was purchased by Henry Gladwin in 1724. The house is believed to be c1700 and although accredited to William Smith there is no evidence that it is his work. The rear is older than the classic front portion. It's slightly wider with different

THE SIDE VIEW OF STUBBING COURT SHOWING THE OLDER REAR SECTION

fenestration and no parapet.

The front portion is accredited to Major-General Henry Gladwin who acquired the estate from his father in 1765. Major Gladwin was the hero of the siege of Detroit in 1763 against the Indian leader Pontiac. A local legend tells how the whole garrison would have been wiped out if an Indian squaw who had made moccasins for the General hadn't warned him of the intended attack.

The house remained in the Gladwin family passing to Lieutenant Colonel Charles Dakeyne Gladwin, then his widow who married the Rev. Immanuel Halton, rector of South Wingfield. Direct descents of the Gladwin line died out in the next generation and continued through the children of Frances, sister of Charles Dakeyne Gladwin. Married to Francis Goodwin, their son the Rev. Henry Goodwin was left most of his uncle's estate including Stubbing Court. His son Richard Henry Goodwin took the name Goodwin-Gladwin.

For the vast part of the nineteenth century, the property was let to such notable names as the Rt. Hon. James Abercrombie, later to be created Lord Dunfermline, at that time Speaker of the House of Commons; Jonathan Thompson, Receiver General of the land revenues for the Crown for the eight Northern Counties; Thomas Humphrey Pedley. Charles Seeley M.P.; Simon Manlove, Holymoorside cotton mill owner; and the Soames family.

HAROLD SOAMES
MEETS KATHARINE HILL

KATHARINE HILL, OLAVE'S MOTHER

Katharine Mary Hill was extremely elegant and beautiful. Of aristocratic lineage, she was the great, great grand-daughter of the 7th Earl of Kinnoul and could trace her ancestors back to the late 15th century.

But the family fortunes changed around 1880 when Katharine's father had the misfortune to lose all his money. It was then necessary for his daughters to find gainful employment, not an easy task for girls of gentle birth. The choices were very limited and usually centred around domestic life, as governesses or companions.

Annette and Gertude (Olave's god-mother) became art teachers; Annette at Rugby School, and Gertrude at Bilton Grange, the prep. school for Rugby School. Marion married. Constance started a girls' school at Halliwick in Hertfordshire and Katharine, after a short period as a governess in Switzerland became a companion to a London family.

The family consisted of four children, two of school age and two older. When in February 1883 the older son Chris brought home a friend for lunch Katharine recognised him as a brother of Reginald Soames who she had met some years previously. His name was Harold Soames and in her diary Katharine wrote:

'this man was very bright and genial and made a pleasant addition to our luncheon party.'

A few months later, the family decided to move to Malta, and Katharine had the predicament of finding another position. But fate was to intervene. Before leaving, a farewell dinner was given and Harold Soames was invited. He had become infatuated by Katharine and the following morning he proposed, she accepted and they were married on December 20th 1883 at Trinity Church, Paddington. She was thirty two, he was twenty nine.

Katharine kept a diary, a large handwritten volume bound in red morocco leather, and as Harold was an excellent painter, he illustrated it with charming little water-colours. The diary gives a deep insight into Katharine's character and her gift for self-drama-tisation. When describing her new husband she wrote:

HAROLD SOAMES

'on the border line of genius, cynical, exacting, pessimistic and keenly critical; mitigated by an intellect of singular brilliance. His mental culture, his sense of beauty, his love of nature, his power of giving out from a richly-stored mind that is equally willing to take in, makes him a companion of peculiar charm and interest.'

The diary also contains detailed descriptions and stories of their life-style and the early life of their children. In 1904, Katharine copied it out three times, and presented one to each of her children.

I am grateful that when I was working on *The Derbyshire Childhood of Olave, Lady Baden-Powell G.B.E.*, Lady Patience Baden-Powell, allowed me to read and use extracts from this amazing journal that are included here.

1890 Stubbing
moor. Reluctantly, we realise changes
that must be made before long.
A change at Brampton is compelled
by an agreement, which gives H's
partner the option to buy out or leave.
And should he be the one to stay there
must be a change of house
In any case, Stubbing passes into
new hands. — & our life here will roll
into the mists of the past. ——

The weird lonesome day of my
home coming — The happy advent of
each dear child —— The links that
are forged in our minds with the
scene of our children's first
years — our life in the middle
Valley will ever remain with us
a golden memory & through all
change & changes of the future,
we shall retain in our hearts the
picture of Old Stubbing standing
grey & desolate below the sunsets
crimson glow on stone edge or
half hidden by snow drifts through
long months of silence.

A PAGE FROM KATHARINE SOAMES' DIARY

THE SOAMES FAMILY HOME
STUBBING COURT, WINGERWORTH

STUBBING COURT; AN EARLY PHOTOGRAPH
TAKEN TOWARDS THE END OF THE 19TH CENTURY

Katharine and Harold Soames made their first home together at Stubbing Court. This delightful country estate, even today is set in a quiet valley with pleasant hill and woodland scenery. For Katharine, used to the noise and bustle of London it must have been extremely quiet and rather lonely. Harold hadn't really used the house which Katharine described as big and gloomy. In her diary she wrote how she opened up long closed rooms to fresh air, rooms that were *'gasping for sunshine'*. The only staff consisted of an old man and woman with a young girl employed when necessary.

Riding was still the able-bodied persons mode of transport, and every day Harold would ride the four miles to the brewery leaving Katharine to spend her days in seclusion.

As the news of their marriage began to circulate, Katharine wrote in her diary:

> *'ladies of high and low degree trickle out from Chesterfield and beyond to see what manner of woman has disturbed the hermit of Stubbing.'*

On September 26th 1885, Katharine gave birth to a daughter who was given the family name of Auriol, and the following year on October 11th 1886, a son Arthur Granville was born.

It must have been a very lonely life for a young woman who on her doctor's advice, accepted that the normal treatment for a pregnant lady of her station must be six months resting on a sofa. Extracts from Katharine's diary show that she did not always adhere to this advice.

In January 1889 whilst returning home late one afternoon over Bolehill, a desolate area of uninhabited countryside bordering onto the Stubbing Court land, she fell at a stile. Being eight months pregnant she was understandably upset and fearful of any possible damage done to her unborn child.

Her anxiety turned to terror as on the evening of February 21st, Katharine started in labour. Assisted by a doctor and a nurse, two lives hung in the balance but in the pearly grey light of a cool February dawn, a tiny baby girl was born.

Katharine's diary entry dated February 22nd 1889 reads:

> *'The dawn breaks on a new life nearly extinct and I am saved to love and welcome my tiny babe Olave. My heart goes out to this little daughter – the token of a life spared, of dead hopes revived. If I can rear her – if this tiny, frail creature, with all loving care survives the dangers of her birth, and her presence be linked ever with the heaviness that endured for a night, may the clear course of her life be associated with the joy that came in the morning.'*

Olave did survive and the only reference in the diary for the next few months stated that she slept like a little dormouse, wrapped in flannel in the nursery over the briar garden.

A COPY OF THE BIRTH CERTIFICATE OF OLAVE ST. CLAIR SOAMES

In April she was christened Olave St. Clair Soames by her mother's brother who was curate of the parish church of Buxted in Sussex. The name Olive means peace and joy, but the spelling of Olave was her father's choice, because he loved the stirring Norse sagas. If Olave had been a boy his name would have been Olaf. Olave's second name St. Clair was after her godmother, Gertrude St. Clair Hill.

1889

Apart from 1889 being the year that Olave St. Clair Soames was born, what else was happening?

Queen Victoria was on the throne of England, having two years previously celebrated her Jubilee Year – fifty years of a reign that marked a period of almost unbroken peace, growing prosperity and social reforms. The nation as a whole had a strong and lasting affection for their sixty nine year old monarch who at this time had been a widow for twenty eight years.

There was a lull in the African wars. The Eiffel Tower was

completed in Paris in May, New York had its first sky-scraper, a thirteen storey building on Broadway, and the London Savoy Hotel opened on August 6th.

Lord Salisbury was Conservative Prime Minister, the Labour Party was still in its infancy and the standard rate of income tax was six pence in the pound.

Riding was still the able-bodied persons mode of transport with horse drawn coaches, carriages, and donkey carts. Canals linked rivers forming a navigable water system for increased trade, while steam as a motive power was revolutionizing transport by land and sea. Navvies were laying railway lines across the country and one of the greatest pioneers of the railway boom was George Stephenson. He lived the latter part of his life in Chesterfield and in 1848 was buried in Holy Trinity church, Newbold. Air ships and balloons weren't exactly dominating the skies, but it would be fourteen more years before the Wright Brothers were to fly a heavier than air machine.

Motoring was making big strides in Germany and France but was hampered in Britain by the Red Flag Act which restricted speeds to 4 mph on country roads and 2mph in towns. The Act was not repealed until 1896.

In 1885 J.K. Starley had invented the chain driven bicycle, followed in 1887 by Dunlop inventing the pneumatic tyre, but cycling was still in its infancy.

Gas provided lights, and the 'wash down' toilet, similar to our modern flush was invented. This was to replace the earth closet but not for many years. There were no vacuum cleaners, no cinemas and no radios. It would be another nine years before Marconi sent and received his first wireless signal across the channel, and the tone quality of early gramophones meant that they were used for nothing more exalted than comic songs.

Changes were also taking place at the brewery and in 1889, the partnership of Chater and Soames was dissolved. This was due to an earlier agreement made between Harold and his partner, giving Chater the option to buy out or leave. Chater elected to bid the brewery farewell and could hardly conceal his satisfaction in leaving what he believed to be a sinking ship. Harold Soames

AN EARLY ADVERTISING POSTER FOR THE BRAMPTON BREWERY

became sole proprietor and the name was changed to The Brampton Brewery Company.

The extra work and financial strain stretched Harold to the limit and according to Katharine, he *'had to cope single handed with the sordid struggle of a commercial world'*. He did in fact have a manager named William Charlsworth and a chief brewer named Walter John Wilkinson, and together they set about expanding trade and increasing brewing capacity. They outed the antiquated equipment and created a state of the art enterprise using steam power to hoist materials and to pump water and wort, the sweet liquid obtained from the soaked mixture of warm water and ground malt, to the required points in the production process.

Harold was working long hours and the added distance from his home to the brewery daily only added to the pressure. Coupled with this was the loneliness felt by Katharine with her young family living in such an isolated spot, so they decided to look around for a suitable house within a short distance of the brewery.

The house they chose was West House, West Bars, Chesterfield, bought by private treaty in September 1889.

The Derbyshire Times – Saturday September 21st 1889 states:

> '*I much regret to hear on high authority that Mr Edmund Anthony Jefferson Maynard J.P., C.C. of West House, Chesterfield has sold his mansion and grounds to Mr Harold Soames of Stubbing Court and will shortly leave Chesterfield.*'

The Derbyshire Courier – Saturday November 23rd 1889 ran a letting advertisement by Shipton, Hallewell & Co. Solicitors, Chesterfield.

> *To Let; For Entry at Lady Day Next*
>
> *The Mansion House called Stubbing Court with the Flower and Kitchen Gardens and Grounds &c.*
>
> *The house contains Entrance Hall, Library, Two Anti-Rooms, Drawing Room, Dining Room, Back Hall, Good Kitchen, Butler's Pantry, Servant's Hall, Wash House, Brew House &c.*
>
> *The outside premises comprise Coach House, Gig House, Stabling for Six Horses, Hay Chambers, Harness Room and other usual Out Offices.*
>
> *The Gardens are very good and include Vinery and Conservatory &c and the House and Grounds comprise over Four Acres.*
>
> *The House stands in a well-wooded Park and in a most picturesque situation with beautiful views and is about three miles from Chesterfield, a first class station on the Main Midland, and the same distance from Ashover.*
>
> *There is also a station on the Midland Main Line at Clay Cross, two miles from the house.*
>
> *The shooting over the estate of over 500 acres, with a good Wood, goes with the House.*
>
> *For Rent and Particulars, apply to George Oates, Land Agent, Chesterfield or to Shipton, Hallewell & Co., Solicitors, Chesterfield.*

This obviously attracted the attention of another Chesterfield Brewer, Mr Samuel Burkitt J.P. who had joined the Chesterfield Brewery Co as a partner in 1875. He bought the freehold of Stubbing Court which passed to his son William Burkitt who died,

according to reports, Chesterfield's wealthiest bachelor. Succession passed to his nearest relative Colonel Humble Burkitt who returned from Australia to live at Stubbing Court.

Katharine's diary records the great sadness that the Soames family felt leaving Stubbing Court:

'Stubbing passes into new hands – our life here will roll into the mists of the past. The weird lonesome day of my homecoming – the happy event of each dear child – the links that are forged in our minds with the scene of our children's first years – our life in this middle valley will ever remain with us, a golden memory.

Through all change and changes of the future, we shall retain in our hearts the picture of old Stubbing standing grey and desolate below the sun sets crimson glow on Stanedge, or half hidden by snow drifts through long months of silence.

Like ants we carry our most precious treasures bit by bit in our hands, to the new house – and having made ready charming nurseries, I drive the little carriage out to bring my babies from Stubbing – as a defiance of the tears that arise, we leave in apparent indifference.'

WEST HOUSE, WEST BARS, CHESTERFIELD

At the beginning of the Victorian ages, rich and poor alike lived within the small, central area of Chesterfield. Moorland areas and open aspects were found close to the town's boundaries on most approaches and the view of the town from the heights on all sides

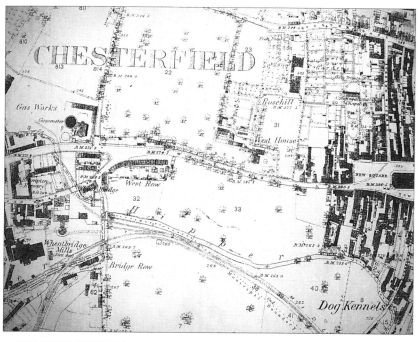

THE FIRST STREET MAP OF CHESTERFIELD – 1876. WEST HOUSE IS IN THE CENTRE, SURROUNDED BY MEADOWS, WHILE OVER ON THE LEFT, HARDLY FIVE MINUTES WALK AWAY IS THE BRAMPTON BREWERY

MAYNARD'S MEADOW LOOKING TOWARDS WEST BARS AND CHESTERFIELD.
ROSE HILL IS ON THE LEFT AND NEXT TO IT IS WEST HOUSE

AN EARLY LITHOGRAPH DATED 1849 SHOWS CHESTERFIELD FROM THE FIELDS
OF BOYTHORPE. IRONICALLY THIS LOCATION IS NOW BADEN-POWELL ROAD
BUT THE VIEW HAS CHANGED OUT OF ALL RECOGNITION. THE CROOKED
SPIRE, STILL CHESTERFIELD'S MOST RECOGNISED LANDMARK IS OVER ON THE
RIGHT. WEST HOUSE IS ON THE EXTREME LEFT BACKED BY TREES AND FRONT-
ED BY MAYNARD'S MEADOW

was of a community clustered around the great St. Mary and All Saints Church with its famous crooked spire. Despite the inevitable industrial development that has taken place, the town is still surrounded by some of the most lovely and unspoilt countryside.

In the late Victorian period, prosperous families lived in spacious houses with tree filled estates set within the town. These individual mansions with their formidable stone walls and carriage entrances allowed their owners to enjoy a country house mode of life within the boundaries of the borough.

One such mansion was West House, situated within a stone's throw of the Market Place yet within easy walking distance of the Brampton Brewery.

The drive to West House entered the property through stone gate posts on West Bars, the street leading from the south-west corner of New Square to the Borough of Brampton. New Square in those days was nothing more than a marshy patch of land used for common grazing and much loved by many local pigs which earned it the name Swine's Green.

WEST BARS LOOKING TOWARDS THE TOWN.
THE WALL SURROUNDING WEST HOUSE IS OVER ON THE LEFT

The origin of the name West Bars is attributed to two large, rude, wooden posts which formerly stood on opposite sides of this road. We still have West Bars on this western approach to the town, but East Bars which stood at the entrance to Vicar Lane is long forgotten. It is thought that a bar or gate extended between the posts in order to prevent cattle straying into the town before the land on the outskirts was enclosed. Below the market place was Toll Nook where livestock would be penned either before or after the herders paid the fee for entering through the east or west bars.

The earliest portion of West House was built in the early years of the eighteenth century. Nearly a century later, Anthony Lax Maynard, a leading citizen of the town was credited with extending the house which passed through generations of the Maynards until Edmund Anthony Jefferson Maynard inherited the mansion and grounds in 1885. He subsequently sold it to Harold Soames in 1889.

West House was a commodious three storey, brick building with a high pedimented stone surround to the front door. The frontal elevation had five bays, the centre three protruded slightly under a low pitched gable, fronted by a triangular pediment. Set in this pediment was an oval plaque carved in stone, a representation of a plum pudding on a dish, symbolically showing the hospitality that might be enjoyed in this house.

Directly opposite West House, although separated by West Bars, was an expanse of meadow land known as Maynard's Meadow. This area was part of the Maynard estate and was officially called West Park. The River Hipper flowed through Maynard's Meadow and over on its eastern boundary was an area known as the Dog Kennels, lying between Low Pavement and the river. This was another area of light industry and cramped, overcrowded, unsanitary housing. Of these forgotten industries, of note was Mason's tobacco cutting factory, Holland's Lace Mill and a flourish business making beaver hats.

Alderman T.P. Wood was elected to the Chesterfield Town Council at the age of 23, was Mayor three times and gave 45 years of continuous service to the town. During his 1886 manorial year he had the idea to provide a public park to celebrate the Golden Jubilee

ONE OF THE EARLIEST PHOTOGRAPHS OF CHESTERFIELD TAKEN IN THE 1870'S
SHOWING THE RIVER HIPPER FLOWING THROUGH MAYNARD'S MEADOW AND
LOOKING TOWARDS THE AREA KNOW AS THE DOG KENNELS. ON THE SKY LINE
IS THE MARKET HALL

of Queen Victoria in 1887. The scheme was approved following a
public meeting on March 31st 1887, and the chosen site was
Maynard's Meadow which was purchased by public subscription.

QUEEN'S PARK, CHESTERFIELD

THE BANDSTAND IS A TRIBUTE TO ALDERMAN WOOD

The formal dedication of the park was made on September 21st 1887, and the same year, Alderman Wood was made a Freeman of the Borough. The Park covered twenty two acres and proved to be such a popular venue that a further five acres were purchased in October 1889. This enabled a boating lake, bandstand, cycle track and gymnasium to be added, and a football and cricket ground to be laid out. The bandstand is a tribute to Alderman Wood.

Queen's Park as it became known was officially opened in August 1893. The first cricket match was played in the Park on May 5th 1894, and the first county cricket match followed in June 1898. A further 13 acres of land were purchased and opened as an Annexe in 1901.

THE SOAMES FAMILY HOME
WEST HOUSE, CHESTERFIELD

WEST HOUSE, WEST BARS, CHESTERFIELD

In April 1890, the Soames family moved into West House and it became their home for five years. Katharine's diary records:

> 'West House is a delightful sun trap – facing south and though its entrance is actually in the town of Chesterfield, we see nothing that jars save a few chimneys through the trees looking towards Brampton.
>
> On the west side from the dining room and from my room over-

head and the nursery above that, we can see the distant moors and white road that winds away to Chatsworth.'

Inside the house, the High Victorian look that can best be described as over-decoration still dominated. Elaborate ornamentation was beloved by the Victorians but this was the era of William Morris, the introduction of mass produced wallpapers, and the Arts and Crafts movement with its cleaner lighter lines which would have better suited Katharine's elegant taste. In her diary she wrote:

'Inside the house is a square, broad staircase and rooms with hideous decoration.'

The fine bay window of the dining room at West House looked west over the garden. Here it forms the background for this family group photographed in 1890.

Olave St. Clair Soames aged fifteen months is on the knee of her Godmother Miss Josephine Gillstrap. Others in the group are – seated left to right Miss Gertude Hill, Olave's aunt and Godmother, Olave and Miss Josephine Gillstrap, Mrs Katharine Soames, mother; Miss Drummond Hay, cousin, and Mrs Watson, aunt. Sister Auriol aged four and three year old brother Arthur share the floor with their father Mr Harold Soames and Bonnie the collie.

According to Olave's autobiography, she remembered how from the vantage point of their nursery window, Arthur, Auriol and she used to watch the horse fairs that took place across in Maynard's Meadow. They no doubt also watched the horse drawn coaches, the carriages, and tramcars that passed along West Bars.

The first scheme to operate horse drawn tramcars in Chesterfield was approved in 1879, and after set-backs and delays, the first section of tramway from Brampton passing along West Bars to the Market Hall was opened on November 8th 1882.

In her diary, Katharine mentions the tram-lines etched in the surface of the road along West Bars:

'Across a hidden road with tram lines, we look to open grounds and fields.'

NUMBER 8 – THE ORIGINAL HORSE-DRAWN TRAM PHOTOGRAPHED ON WEST BARS AT THE JUNCTION WITH CLARENCE ROAD C 1882-1897

The service started operating with three vehicles, two being double deck and one single seating thirty two and eighteen passengers respectively. In 1890 a further two single deck trams were added. One of the earliest horse-drawn trams, No 8 – was saved and after extensive restoration in 1982, placed on loan to the National Tramway Museum at Crich, Derbyshire.

Because there were no loops or turntables to enable the trams to turn round for their return journey, they had bodies which swivelled about a central pivot while the truck remained in the tracks. In order to do this, the horses while still in the shafts, were trained to side-step until the carriage was turned to face the opposite direction.

Horse power was the normal mode of transport at the turn of the century and in 1891, Katharine's diary records:

'A cob is bought to go with out existing horse and my little chaise is changed for a carriage that plays many parts. Harold has also got for me a little cart that takes us far and near.'

There were frequent visits to Stubbing Court.

'The new owners of Stubbing are friendly and allow the Soames to visit and the children to play in the grounds. We bring Olave some-times and I am amused at the patronising air of the others because she is too little to remember – though with the confidence of two – she says she does.'

At the brewery, shire horses, noted for their great strength and size were used to pull the drays to deliver the ales and stouts. As a special treat, Olave was taken to the brewery, or on their day of rest to the fields behind the Terminus Hotel at Brampton – now the playing fields of Brookfield School – almost one and a half miles along Chatsworth Road. She was lifted up level with the large kindly eyes of these gentle natured giants, to stroke their big, broad heads.

In 1892, Brampton Brewery had twenty two horses, and land adjoining the brewery was acquired for building extra stabling. At its peak, thirty five horses worked at the brewery.

A GROUP OF BRAMPTON BREWERY EMPLOYEES 1892

Deliveries were made to high class premises and low class beer houses, as well as private houses. Horse draymen delivering to the tied houses could expect a customary drink at each, and often, in an intoxicated state they fell asleep at the reigns, relying upon the horse to continue the round and get them safely home again.

Drinking water at the time was unclean and beer or ale was drunk as a substitute because the brewing process removed bacteria and impurities. In its heyday, the weekly output at Brampton Brewery was 30,000 gallons of high quality beer with the idiosyncratic local characteristics which now make regional beers so popular. Employees were allowed two free pints per day and all visitors were allowed a free drink whilst there too. The brewery had its own bottling plant, and in 1893, a wine, spirit and cigar department was added.

Considering that West House was almost in the heart of the town, behind the high stone walls were extensive grounds which boasted a stable block, hot houses, walled gardens and an orchard where the Soames children played. Each had a little garden where

they tended their favourite flowers.
Katharine's diary records:

'In great triumph, tiny bunches of first blooms are brought for my gracious acceptance.'

The orchard was also the roaming ground of the hens that were looked after by Katharine and the children. Later the entire enterprise of caring for the hens was passed to Olave and Auriol. They were responsible for buying food, breeding, rearing and selling eggs. It was a good way to master maths on a practical level, a

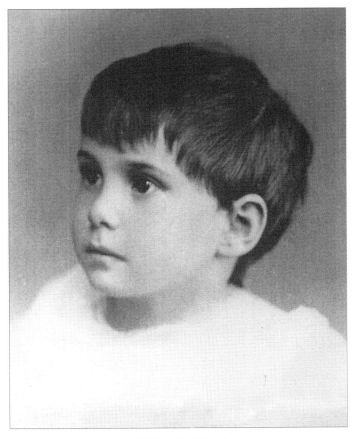

OLAVE AGED THREE

subject Olave hated in the classroom.

Arthur and Auriol received lessons at home and as Olave became old enough she joined them in the classroom. They were taught by a succession of nannies and nursery governesses both English and French, including Berthe, Louise and Wissie. As Berthe *'reached the end of her tether'*, she left and was replaced by Louise who in turn left quite abruptly. Miss Wilson, affectionately known as Wissie was their first real Governess and stayed for two and a half years.

Katharine's diary entry records finding Miss Wilson in May 1893:

'Olave in her big sun-bonnet, little legs straight out – by my side in the Phaeton, chatters all the way to Mansfield where we are chasing a Governess. We run her to ground at the High School, Mansfield.'

Olave was four when Wissie joined the family. Arthur and Auriol now began regular lessons and Olave joined them for walks. She delighted in the stories that Wissie was always ready to tell them.

Katharine was also delighted with Wissie and her diary entry for August 1893 says:

'Confidence in Miss Wilson who has succeeded Louise grows with her increasing influence with each child. Feeling they are safe in her charge, we accept an invitation to stay with the W.T.'s in Yorkshire for the grouse shooting. We join the children with Wissie at York and proceed to Whitby for September.'

Changes were taking place in Maynard's Meadow. The area below the Midland Railway, Brampton Branch line (later to be the route of Markham Road) was being transformed into Queen's Park. The River Hipper was being diverted but the land between West Bars and the Midland branch line to Brampton was acquired by the Lancashire, Derbyshire and East Coast Railway to build their headquarters and terminus, impinging upon the open aspect of West House. The Chesterfield section of the railway with its terminus at the Market Place station, was completed in 1897 and at this time, West Bars was widened and improved to meet the

THE NEW LANCASHIRE, DERBYSHIRE AND EAST COAST RAILWAY
STATION BUILT DIRECTLY OPPOSITE WEST HOUSE

demands of increasing traffic and provide better access to the new railway station.

Katharine's diary records:

> *Business improves steadily and five years of hard toil have set the ship on calmer seas. Harold begins to reap the fruits of his labours – his daily presence is not now imperative – so for our children's sake, we are tempted to sell West House and move again to the country.*
>
> *The Terminus of a new railway is being made in front of our house which increases the value of the land, and Harold sells it well.'*

West House retained its use as a private residence until on Saturday, March 23rd 1907, after a large scheme of re-decoration, it opened its doors to the general public as The Park Hotel & Restaurant, an unlicensed commercial and visitors house.

A report in the *Derbyshire Times* dated March 16th 1907 records the event.

WEST HOUSE, CHESTERFIELD
NEW DEVELOPMENTS CHANGE THE CHARACTER
OF AN OLD CHESTERFIELD MANSION

Saturday of next week will see the passing of an old country residence West

43

House which has been claimed for business extensions and becomes the Park Hotel. To the older people of Chesterfield, the change recalls much of Chesterfield in the past, the days when the railway had not pierced to this end of town, and the West Park, now entirely built over, was an expanse of green fields.

But the old state of things will soon have passed away. The coach house which in years gone by has sheltered many a fine carriage, will in the future do similar duty to the modern motor car, and 'Maynard's Plum Pudding' high on the front of the building may still be looked upon as an invitation to accept the hospitality of the house although now in a commercial sense.

It is intended to make it a large unlicensed commercial and visitors' house, and a large scheme of decoration has been undertaken.

By an ingenious plan of sub-division, there are now in all twenty six bedrooms and near to the dining and smoking rooms on the ground floor, the restaurant will be placed. This is lighted by a fine bay window facing the lawn, which in summer will probably be the scene for many al fresco dinners.

In the restaurant it may be noted, are a very beautiful pair of alcoves and a door decorated, after a design by Flaxman.With the introduction of electric light, the preparation of the gardens and the furnishing of the house on the most modern lines, every effort is being made to perfect the arrangements before the opening day. Nothing that modernity can do short of absolute re-construction will remove from the place the 'country house' appearance which strikes the visitor first.

With the house practically on the doorstep of the Market Place station of the Great Central (late Lancashire, Derbyshire and East Coast Railway) there ought to be plenty of attraction here for visitors.

West House, West Bars, Chesterfield 1894

A PAINTING OF WEST HOUSE BY COL. J. KINSMAN WHOSE RELATIVES, THE BARNES FAMILY MOVED IN AFTER THE SOAMES FAMILY MOVED OUT
Chesterfield Library

44

WEST HOUSE IN THE CENTRE OF THIS PHOTOGRAPH TAKEN AT THE TURN OF
THE LAST CENTURY. THE SIDINGS OF THE LANCASHIRE,
DERBYSHIRE AND EAST COAST RAILWAY ARE IN THE FOREGROUND

WEST HOUSE BECAME THE PARK HOTEL AND RESTAURANT IN 1907

THE ENTRANCE TO WEST HOUSE ON THE LEFT,
LOOKING TOWARDS THE TOWN

THE DEMOLITION OF WEST HOUSE AND ROSE HILL

WEST HOUSE WAS DEMOLISHED IN 1936

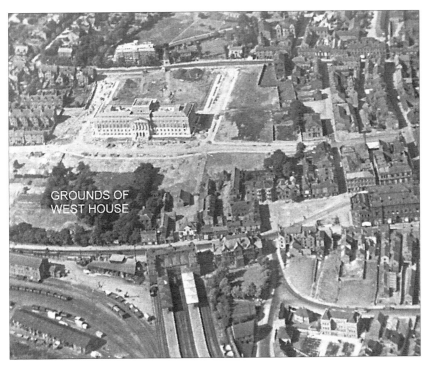

THIS MAGNIFICENT AERIAL VIEW FROM THE 1930'S SHOWS THE NEWLY BUILT
TOWN HALL IN THE CENTRE. BELOW, THE GROUNDS OF WEST HOUSE ARE
STILL INTACT ALTHOUGH THE BUILDING HAS GONE

TAKEN FROM THE SAME VIEW POINT, WEST BARS WITH A CENTURY BETWEEN. THE SITE OF WEST HOUSE IS NOW SHENTALL GARDENS THE SITE OF THE LANCASHIRE, DERBYSHIRE & EAST COAST RAILWAY SHEDS IS NOW C.P.P. AND POST OFFICE COUNTER SERVICES

The Lancashire, Derbyshire and East Coast Railway fared very little better. Although it was planned to link Warrington to Sutton on Sea thus the name, the scheme was a financial disaster and only the Chesterfield to Lincoln section was completed. That would probably account for why it changed its name to the Great Central Railway, as the Chesterfield station was actually its terminus. The line built up a considerable traffic in coal, but the passenger business was never great.

In 1948 the Lancashire, Derbyshire and East Coast Railway by then known as the Great Central, mounted an exhibition to commemorate the Centenary of George Stephenson's death. To mark the opening of Chesterfield's Centenary fortnight, a wreath was placed by the Mayor on Stephenson's tomb near the altar of Holy Trinity Church, Newbold.

The last passenger train ran from the Market Place station of the LD&EC Railway on December 3rd 1951 but the line remained open for freight until March 4th 1957 when it finally closed.

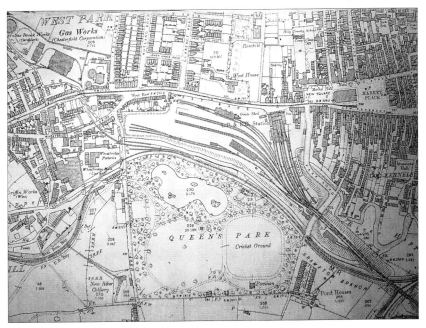

THE SECOND EDITION OF THE CHESTERFIELD STREET MAP c1898

THE OLD STATION BUILDING IN THE LATE 1960's SHOWING ITS CLOSE PROXIMITY TO THE PORTLAND HOTEL IN THE FOREGROUND, AND THE TOWERING AGD BLOCK (SINCE DEMOLISHED)

The station building which stood next door to the Portland Hotel and directly opposite the Sun Inn, was then occupied by Stanton's Paint and Wallpaper Company until the building was demolished in 1972. Now no trace of the LC & EC Railway remains in the town. The site is part of the Portland Hotel car park and a new stretch of road that sweeps round from West Bars into New Beetwell Street.

The area that was once covered by the railway sidings is now covered by the massive office buildings of the C.P.P. and Post Office Counters known as Number 1 Future Walk.

THE SOAMES FAMILY HOME RENISHAW HALL, ECKINGTON

The literary fame of the Sitwells is international yet their roots in North Derbyshire can be traced back to 1301. Their family home is Renishaw Hall standing aloof on the edge of the village of Eckington where pastoral charm and Victorian industry merge. Only over the hill to the north are the sprawling housing developments and industrial lands of Sheffield.

The centre core of Renishaw Hall around which the present Hall has grown, was built in the early seventeenth century. One and a half centuries later, Sir Sitwell Sitwell completed many additions

RENISHAW HALL PHOTOGRAPHED AT THE TURN OF LAST CENTURY

and alterations, extending the Hall to three times its original size. By the turn of the nineteenth century, the Hall was almost as we see it today.

Approached through gates in the village of Eckington, the drive rises and dips over the golf course and through the park. The northern elevation visible from this side is three storeys high, long and bleak. It is topped with a castellated parapet despite its Georgian windows.

Passing round the Hall, its southern elevation gives a totally different face, surrounded by delightful gardens and enjoying superb views over the valley of the River Rother.

Katharine's diary records:

'Harold has sometimes, while waiting for a train, strolled up Eckington station to refresh himself with a sight of Sir George Sitwell's lovely place, Renishaw – to him a place of dreams and delight. Though only seven miles from Chesterfield I have never seen it, and when the agent, an artist friend of Harolds offers to let to him this beautiful Renishaw, the heavens are opened and a dream is realised.'

Sir George Reresby Sitwell, 4th Baronet of Renishaw nicknamed Ginger, was twice returned as Conservative M.P. for Scarborough. While the Sitwell family resided at Scarborough, Renishaw Hall was leased to the Soames family for two years.

Katharine's diary records the delight Harold found in the gardens:

'Harold has inherited from some horticultural ancestor, not only a tendency to weed which stood him in good stead at Stubbing, but also a true love of gardening.

He rejoices in the possibilities of these well planned gardens and sets vigorously to work at a pace that lends itself to his higher schemes.'

For temporary periods when the Sitwell family moved back to Renishaw, they offered the Soames family their home in Scarborough.

Katharine's diary entry 1895 records:

'The Sitwells again change houses with us in August – and this time we take carriages and horses to enjoy the drives round Scarborough.'

It may have been the delight of exploring Renishaw or the excitement of a proposed long stay at Scarborough that caused Olave aged six to suffer a near fatal fall over the stair banisters. Katharine's diary records:

'Our luggage has gone and I await the children with Madame in the hall. A distant excited chatter and two wild things fly downstairs screaming incoherent tidings about Olave falling over the stairs on to a sky-light. I find my little one insensible with a gash on her head – someone flies for a doctor and half senseless myself, I bath the

ghastly wound and hold the limp little body – scarcely breathing – while weeping children are soothed outside.

How the child fell over – how she can have jumped high enough in her excitement to overbalance herself is a mystery – we can only gather that the others heard a crash and rushing back Auriol clung to Olave's legs through the rail – and saved her from a hideous fall of thirty feet to a stone floor below.

The screams quickly brought help. The good doctor came at once and dressed and stitched and pronounced concussion and quiet and darkness. So, I hurried off Madame with the two distressed children in time to catch their train – anxiously watching my little invalid in the still house alone with a faithful maid.

I awaited the advance guard of the Sitwells with a large house party.

I shall never forget the wonderful kindness I received from Sir George and his wife and each of their guests. From the room where I watched my child day and night – I heard no sound and could not have believed the great house held a soul but ourselves in that dark chamber – and the maid who crept silently by to wait upon us.'

THE RENISHAW GHOST

TAKEN FROM THE GHOST HUNTERS GAME BOOK

What stately home would be complete without its ghosts and Renishaw is no exception. This story is included here as a follow-up to Olave's accident on the staircase. Was it caused by something more than childish high spirits?

You can be the judge!

In 1885, when Sir George had his coming of age party there was a large house party at RenishawHall. Guests included the Archbishop of Canterbury, Dr Tait and his daughter. Miss Tait was given a room at the top of the staircase. She woke up in the middle of the night trembling with fright, because someone had given her three cold kisses.

She ran through into the bedroom of Sir George's sister, woke her and told Miss Sitwell what had happened.Having listened to the story, she said that she had had exactly the same experience herself when she slept in that room at the top of the stairs.

Miss Sitwell made up a temporary bed on a sofa in her room, and Miss Tait spent the rest of the night there.

Next day, Mr Turnbull, the estate agent came up to the house. Sir George told him what had happened to Miss Tait and laughed about it.

Mr Turnbull turned pale and said: 'Well Sir George, you may joke about it, but when you lent us the house for our honeymoon, Miss Crane the sister of Walter Crane the artist, who was at school with my wife, came to stay with us. She had the same room and the same experience.'

Some time after this, Sir George decided to rebuild the staircase and make it larger. His cousin, Mr F.I.Thomas suggested that he should knock down one wall of the room in question and throw it and the room below into the staircase.

Before the work started, Sir George who was going away, told his Clerk of the Works that if they found anything of interest between the floor and the ceiling of the two rooms, they were to let Mr Thomas know at once.

He gave this order, not because he believed in ghosts but because he wanted to have a detailed note concerning the ancient plan of the house.

Soon after, Mr Thomas got a letter from the Clerk of the Works, saying that they had found something most interesting under the floor of the bedroom in which Miss Tait had slept. Mr Thomas immediately went over to Renishaw to see what it was.

They showed him a coffin of seventeenth century design and workmanship, fastened to the joists under the floor boards by iron cramps. It had no lid. The floor boards had acted as a lid. There were no bones in the coffin, but it had certain definite marks which suggested that it had once contained a body.

Twenty years later, Lady Ida Sitwell, Sir George's wife was lying on a sofa in the upstairs drawing room, talking to friends after dinner. Facing the open door, she saw a grey-haired woman, wearing a white cap and something like a crinoline, walk along the outside corridor with a very slow, furtive, gliding motion as if wishing to escape notice. Lady Sitwell thought it was the housekeeper and called out to her by name. There was no reply.

The figure headed straight towards the head of the old staircase. It vanished within a yard of the spot where the door of the haunted room which had been removed twenty years previously had been.

The whole party searched the hall and upstairs passage but could find no-one.

LIFE FOR THE SOAMES CHILDREN
AT RENISHAW HALL

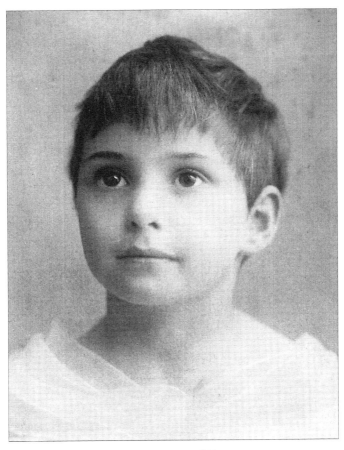

OLAVE AGED SIX

Lessons for the Soames children were taken together that summer until in the Autumn, Arthur was sent off to Bilton, the preparatory school for Rugby.

At the end of 1895, Wissie their beloved governess left and was replaced by a more advance teacher called Miss Heap. She was a disciplinarian, toughened by a sense of duty which did not inspire anything but a school-room attitude in Auriol and Olave. How they envied Arthur, affectionately known as Boogie. In their eyes he had escaped while they were left at home to suffer under Miss Heap who was described as *'toughened by a sense of duty, as practiced by ladies of broad feet and narrow views.'*

Fortunately her reign was short lived and she in turn was replaced by Friede Dentzelmann, a German woman of uncertain age. Her stern demeanour was accentuated by a pair of rimless pince-nez eyeglasses that were held in place by a clip over the bridge of the nose and dangled from a cord when not in use. Her hair was worn pulled back from her face and screwed up into a bun. She was such a disciplinarian that Olave referred to her as a martinet, a person who maintains discipline and power.

Friede kept to a strict routine giving the girls regular lessons in terms, similar to school terms. They worked for one hour before breakfast which was at nine o'clock, then had a walk for an hour before resuming lessons until lunch at one o'clock. Lessons continued from two until four o'clock, tea was at half past four and dinner at seven.

Friede gave them lessons out of doors when the weather was good. She was a fresh-air enthusiast and encouraged, not only lessons out of doors but picnics and expeditions even in winter.

Throughout her childhood, Olave led a real Guide-y lifestyle in the open air, and always maintained that her freedom to revel in the open air in those early days built up a stamina which enabled her to play her part in all weathers at camp rallies. As Baden Powell said many years later, *'it's easy enough to smile and look happy on a sunny day, but it takes a stiff upper lip to keep the smile fixed when the rain is pouring down and the once smart uniform has become sodden and dripping.'*

The cycling craze was reaching a peak, not merely as a means of transport, but as a fashionable pastime, and encouraged by Friede, the girls cycled regularly. They also mastered the art of sailing, handling the little old boat and Sir George's beautiful punt which enabled them to drift lazily across to the island in the lake in the grounds of Renishaw Hall.

THE LAKE IN THE GROUNDS OF RENISHAW HALL

Olave and Auriol never went to school or sat a public examination. The two sisters made their own entertainment and had their own secret society which they called the Bungalow Club. As their governess, Friede lived with the family, travelled around with them and had an enormous influence on Olave during her formative years. Later she became a friend and remained so until her death in 1929.

Both their parents shared a loving if somewhat distant concern for their children and they both believed in learning by doing. An extract from Katharine's diary (or Muz as she was called by the girls) stated that the girls were:

'Untrammelled by any laid down system of education – not made to learn but made to wish to learn in wider spheres of self taught interest.'

Their father taught them to play tennis and later squash. His artistic temperament was displayed in his gardening where he carefully planned colour groupings. He expected help in this from Olave and Auriol who had to learn the names and nature of each flower. As a living memory of their roving life-style, each move saw the removal and re-planting of shrubs and plants –

'that will in strange soil sport into old friends, beginning with the gentians from Stubbing Court,' Katharine wrote.

Katharine was irritated by people who sat with idle hands. She worked wonderful needlework, knitting and crochet, and taught her daughters too. They were expected to sew samplers to show the range of their embroidery skills and with some effort, Olave learnt to knit. Taught by Friede, she learnt the German way of knitting which is much quicker and neater than the English method. Olave became quite proficient although she never made anything larger or more complicated than socks or scarves.

With great determination, she made a comforter for one of the keepers on the Renishaw estate. Having completed her handiwork, she carried the comforter to the old gentleman and proudly gave it to him.

On her return, her mother asked what he had said.

'He said – thank you my little man,' replied Olave, and when her mother asked what she had said to that she replied, 'well, I didn't undeceive him as I thought that might hurt his feelings.'

Making one's own entertainment was very much a part of life at the turn of the century. The familiar routine is outlined in Olave's diary:

'Morning played with hoops, afternoon wet, made camphor bags, evening read and wrote poetry.'

On the whole, Olave was a very happy child although like many children, she sometimes used to sulk. On these occasions Friede would say;

'Oh Susannah is with us today is she? Now then Olave, take Susannah out of the room and leave her there.'

Their parents had few interests in common, although they both enjoyed entertaining. Many evenings the children lay awake in their beds, listening to their parent's musical evenings. Auriol leant to play the piano and Olave the violin. Apparently at Olave's first appearance in public she insisted on playing with her back to the audience to give herself confidence.

Katharine called her first violin 'her first little squeaker'. Olave called it Diana. It was a copy of a Stradivarius made by Messrs Hill for the Paris Exhibition. The family endured the early efforts without discouraging her and Olave's fiddle became a great source of pleasure to her throughout her life. Many years later, Diana was presented to the Guide Association and is still available on loan to Guides who are seriously learning to play the violin prior to them acquiring their own instrument.

KATHARINE AND HAROLD SOAMES WOULD ENTERTAIN
IN THE SPLENDID RECEPTION ROOMS AT RENISHAW HALL

OLAVE AND HER ANIMALS

OLAVE WITH HER BELOVED DOGS, SHOGGY THE ST. BERNARD AND BONNY THE
COLLIE AT RENISHAW HALL

Friede's first impression of Olave was of;

'A small untidy child, dressed in wellington boots and a scarlet tam-o-shanter on her dark tousled head. Everywhere she went, she had a Collie and a St Bernard in tow.'

Olave loved all animals. She would often sit cradling a hen in her arms or with a dove on her head. The doves were allowed to fly free but encouraged to fly down onto Olave's and Auriol's hands when called. The girls buried their noses in the doves soft neck feathers, and all the hens and ducks had names.

An entry in Olave's diary reads:

'Pulley our dear darling tame black leghorn had six babies. We love her and she sits on the swing with us.'

Many years later Olave was to write in *The Guide*:

'As a child I was rather frightened of grown ups. They seemed so different somehow and didn't love rabbits and doves as I did. They just called them animals or birds and didn't want to hold them and hug them as I did.'

In the days before efficient lawn-mowers, meadows took the place of lawns and these were kept short by grazing horses, sheep or cattle. In order to admire the long stretches of meadow land from the house without the problem of inquisitive cattle, a ha-ha was usually installed, but at Renishaw Hall, the grazing land bordered almost directly onto the front drive.

This division was not made evident to the three grazing horses that one day found the front door open and decided to investigate what appeared to them to be a rather splendid stable. Their presence caused quite an uproar in the household much to the delight of Olave and Auriol as they watched the indifferent animals being shooed outside.

A PERIPATETIC CHILDHOOD

RENISHAW HALL

After two years in the wonderful surroundings of Renishaw Hall, it was time for the Soames family to move on again. This time, they were not restricted to living within a short travelling distance of the Brampton Brewery, as Harold Soames sold the brewery in June 1897 and retired. He was to devote the remainder of his life to his hobbies and things that gave him pleasure; shooting, gardening, painting and travel.

The purchase price of Brampton Brewery was set at £320,000 and a public share issue was raised to purchase the brewery, offices, land and stabling together with 142 licensed houses, ten shops, one hundred and forty three cottages and vacant plots of land mainly within twelve miles of the brewery.

Olave was eight when the Soames family left Derbyshire, moving around the country from one stately home to another searching for what her father described as an 'earthly paradise'. It was not an easy task and over the next eleven years, the Soames family had seven country residences and innumerable London homes.

In June 1897, the family moved to a house overlooking Lake Windermere, but that Autumn Katharine and the girls moved to 18, St. James's Place, London, while Harold went off to Italy painting.

Their next move was to Pixton Park, Somerset, but after nine months they moved to a hotel in Bournemouth where they stayed for eight months. Their next move in 1899 was just twenty miles away to Cranbourne Manor in Dorset. Olave was ten and described as rather small and thin for her age. She and Katharine travelled to Cranbourne in the brougham complete with coachman, and Olave's first impressions as they drove up the tree lined drive was of a dark tunnel leading to an enchanted house. Of all the beautiful houses where she had lived as a child, she was to remember Cranbourne Manor as the most beautiful, graceful in design and built of mellow golden stone.

Harold Soames regularly went abroad on painting holidays leaving Katharine and the girls. Olave's days passed in a seemingly endless procession of parties, picnics and outdoor activities shared with her pets, then as her horizons widened, Katharine took her to London. In 1901 Olave went abroad for the first time to Mentone, France with her mother and father. Katharine hated travel and it was one of the few occasions they went abroad as a family.

In December 1901 they moved to Purley Hall, Pangbourne, Berkshire. Friede left the family and all formal education ceased for Olave and Auriol. Olave's education did not perhaps give her the best chance for making good, but education is best judged by its results.

Auriol was seventeen but there was no such thing as a teenager in those days. Children went overnight from being boys and girls to being men and women. It was a very class-conscious time and for girls of a well-to-do background that meant '*coming out*', celebrated with house parties and balls. Auriol '*did the season*' with Katharine taking her off to London while Olave, who much preferred the country, stayed behind with her father. They would cycle and ride together, play tennis and go shooting.

When Harold went off on his painting trips, the house would be shut up and Katharine would take the girls to London. For her fifteenth birthday, Olave was taken to a Henry Wood concert at the Queen's Hall and the Variety Theatre, a mixture of circus, music-hall and straight musical recitals. She was also introduced to the new underground railway network opened in 1890 and called the tube.

In 1903 at the age of fourteen Olave fell in love for the first time. She was to fall in and out of love many times, receiving three proposals of marriage and turning them all down. In her heart of hearts she knew they were not right.

The family's next move in May 1904 was to Luscombe Castle near Dawlish in Devon which Harold rented for a year. It was so near to the sea that Olave learnt to swim and bathed every day. On December 7th 1904 Olave was confirmed by the Bishop of Crediton at St. Gregory's Church, Dawlish. The occasion filled her with awe, and Olave wrote in her diary: '*I am a beast not to think more of religion.*'

Olave was fifteen, 5ft 4ins and weighed 6 stone 8lbs when she had her portrait painted by Nathaniel H.J. Baird in oils. She was so excited when she saw it on display in a London gallery the following year. It now hangs in the Chesterfield Guide Head-quarters. Baird painted another portrait of her in 1912, a watercolour which now hangs at Foxlease, Hampshire where there is also a drawing by Loen Sprinck done in the same year.

In May 1905, the family moved again. This time it was another Devon house called Bradfield and at the same time Harold took a London flat in Kensington Court where Katharine and Auriol could enjoy the round of dances and theatres.

The peripatetic existence must have tried Katharine's patience. The endless packing and repacking even with an army of servants would have been arduous, but Olave loved all the moving and the packing and unpacking.

Katharine wrote in her diary:

'Olave is equal to three charwomen in work and to the whole char race in wits, hurls all her sweet energy and thought into every corner, and masters at once the intricacies of staircase and passage from dungeon to garret'.

In 1906 Harold took Auriol abroad with him for the winter so Olave accompanied Katharine to London. Here she enjoyed concerts and museums, shopping expeditions and tea parties.

Olave had her *'coming out'* in January 1907, being transformed overnight from child to woman, lowering her skirts and putting up her hair. She was almost eighteen. Harold took Auriol off to Cairo and Olave accompanied Katharine to London for two months, before moving from Bradfield to Hardwick in Suffolk. Soon Katharine declared herself 'Suffolkated' at Hardwick and the search was on for yet another home.

In 1908, Harold Soames bought the family's first real home Grey Rigg in Dorset. In the summer of 1909 Olave was unwell and Harold took her on a cruise to Norway in the S.Y. Vectis. She reported in her diary that she had seen her first ice-berg.

Olave was growing increasingly dissatisfied with her meaningless existence and wrote to a London hospital to enquire about training to be a nurse. She was told to train locally, but Katharine would not agree to that, so the matter was dropped. Shortly afterwards Olave became a volunteer, offering what unskilled help she could to invalid children at The Invalid Children's Aid Association who had a seaside convalescent home in Parkstone.

That winter the family moved to Rutland Lodge in Knightsbridge. Olave had been given a Clumber spaniel to replace her beloved Doogy, and known as Doogy II each morning Olave would cross Knightsbridge to exercise him in Hyde Park.

So the days passed in their usual pattern and Olave confided in her diary that she was disenchanted with life. Half a day at the Invalid Children's Aid Society was not enough to satisfy her. Early in 1911 Harold took Auriol to India where from Ceylon she wrote of her engagement to Bob Davidson. They were married in October and four months later Olave and her father set off for Jamaica.

1909. OLAVE AGED 20

A SHIPBOARD ROMANCE

Olave enjoyed a privileged upbringing and on Wednesday January 3rd 1912, Olave and her father set sail from Southampton on the RMS Arcadian. She wrote home to her mother: *'There is only one interesting person on board and that is the Boy Scout Man who is so nice, so modest and sweet.'*

But there was something more – an instant attraction between Lieutenant-General Sir Robert Stephenson Smyth Baden-Powell K.C.B and Olave. Still a bachelor at 55, he had given up hope of finding a companionable partner, but he was captivated by this energetic young woman. She was amazed to find that he remembered seeing her walking her dog Doogy II in Hyde Park, London, two years earlier. Olave was understandably impressed and rather overawed by the disclosure that a distinguished general and founder of the new Scouting Movement should remember her.

Harold Soames and Robert Baden-Powell soon discovered a mutual interest in painting and talked eagerly together. BP was only three years younger than her father, but perhaps their friendship was a smoke-screen. It would not have done for a fifty five year old distinguished general to be caught flirting with a girl of twenty three. But this was no mere flirtation. There were stolen kisses before dawn, little notes posted in a cleat in one of the lifeboats, and secret meetings at pre-arranged points on the boat deck.

Olave later wrote – *'I can't imagine what it was about me that attracted him. He was famous, talented, experienced. I was such an ordinary person, not at all clever, with no experience of life whatsoever.'*

Shipboard romances are notorious but within five days Olave and BP were helplessly, ecstatically in love. They spoke, half in jest, half in earnest of asking Captain Custance of the Arcadian to marry them, because Olave knew there would be opposition from her parents about their thirty two years age difference, and BP had a loyalty to his widowed mother. Their ship-board romance was kept very hush-hush, but when they parted on January 26th he gave her a Scout Thanks Badge which she wore on a fine chain underneath her dress. They had an understanding that some day despite everything they would be together.

Olave was back in England in March after her two month cruise, and ironically it was only a month later on April 15th 1912 that the White Star liner Titanic met its disastrous end on a similar route to that taken by the Arcadian on which Olave, Harold and BP sailed. The largest and finest ship then afloat, while steaming at full speed across the Atlantic on her maiden voyage, struck the submerged part of an iceberg and went to the bottom. Of the 2,224 people on board, 1,513 were lost. This tragedy which shocked the whole world led to considerable improved safety precautions at sea including the institution of the International Ice Patrol charged with the duties of logging and watching ice-bergs in the North Atlantic.

Because of BP's work commitment, they didn't meet again until September 14th although they exchanged numerous letters, sometimes writing several a day, then on September 20th their engagement was announced. It caused a sensation, and even weeks later, the newspapers were still full of gossip about their engagement and speculation about the forthcoming wedding.

There were such statements as – 'a demonstration of scout loyalty will be expected'; 'what part will the boys who owe him allegiance take in the event?'; 'a large muster of scouts will act as a guard of honour'; 'a guard of honour will surround the bride's house and link up with the church'; and 'a great ceremonial of Boy Scouts will be inspected by the bride and groom'. Neither the bride or groom wanted such a show on what to them was their own private, special day, so they decided to marry quickly, quietly and secretly.

On Wednesday October 30th 1912 at 12.45 p.m., weeks before the dates brandied around by the press, Olave St Clare Soames and

AS A BRIDE OLAVE WORE A SIMPLE BLUE COSTUME, BUT WHEN
PRESENTED AT COURT SIX MONTHS LATER ON MAY 7TH 1913 SHE WORE A
GOWN OF WHITE SATIN, EMBROIDERED WITH LEAVES OF
SILVER, AND CARRIED A BOUQUET OF WHITE ROSES

Lieutenant-General Sir Robert Stephenson Smyth Baden-Powell K.C.B were married at St Peter's Church in Parkstone.

The service was brief and simple and although the church bells did ring in honour of the wedding, it was not until they were on the train for London and a weeks honeymoon at Mullion Cove in Cornwall.

Aware that many people were disappointed by their secret wedding, the newly weds held a late reception for family and friends at the Mercer's Hall, London on December 17th.

In January they set off for a belated honeymoon exploring the countryside around Algiers followed by a week's camping expedition in the mountains that edged the Sahara desert. This was a new experience and a complete novelty for Olave who described it as – *delicious fun, living the simple life in the desert sleeping under the stars.* They only had one pan and it had to be used for everything. In her autobiography Olave said how after cooking fish, she had to scrub it out with grass roots and sand before she could boil water to make coffee.

Baden-Powell was happy to report in a letter to his mother that Olave was – *a perfect wonder in camp – a splendid walker, good scout and never loses her way.*

As a wedding present from the Scout Association, every scout in the country contributed one penny, Scoutmasters gave one shilling, and by March 1913 a total sum of £411.14s.1d had been raised. This was sufficient to buy a 20hp, 6 cylinder Standard Landaulette motor car. It was sprayed in scout colours, a very dark green with a fine yellow line running round, the scout badge discreetly painted on the panel and a silver figure of a scout on the bonnet. It became affectionately known as 'B.P.'s Penny Wedding Present'.

Olave settled down to being a wife and mother. Their first home together was a flat at 35 Rutland Court, London but with the news that they were expecting their first child, on April 12th 1913, the Baden-Powells moved to Ewhurst Place in Sussex. The arrival of baby Arthur Robert Peter, born in 1913 coincided with their first wedding anniversary.

OLAVE AND B-P WITH THEIR 'PENNY WEDDING PRESENT'

HOW LORD BADEN POWELL
STARTED THE SCOUT MOVEMENT

Robert Stephenson Smyth Powell was born on February 22nd 1857 in London. His father was the Reverend Baden Powell who already had four teenage children from his second marriage when he married Henrietta Grace Smyth. Robert was the fifth of their seven children. His first two names came from his godfather, Robert

Stephenson, the railway and civil engineer, and his third name was his mother's maiden name. Robert was only three when his father died and as a tribute to him, Henrietta had the family name changed by Royal Licence on April 30th 1902 to Baden-Powell.

In 1876, Robert joined the 13th Hussars in India. In the early 1880s his regiment was posted to the Natal province of South Africa. He was posted to Malta for three years then returned to South Africa prior to the second Boer War of 1899. By this time he had been promoted to be the youngest colonel in the British Army.

He was responsible for organizing frontiersmen to defend Bechuanaland and Matabeleland and in so doing found himself trapped in the Siege of Mafeking with 1,251 newly enlisted and ill-equipped men, when his base was surrounded by 9,000 determined and well-equipped Boers. There are numerous tales of how he kept up morale while continually confusing the besiegers by unexpected moves and stratagems. This enabled his garrison to withstand the siege for 217 days, and the hero of the siege of Mafeking was promoted to Major-General.

Between 1884-1914, he wrote nine military books the first three on the topic, *Reconnaissance and Scouting* (1884) *Cavalry Instruction* 1885, and the splendidly unlikely *Pigsticking and Hoghunting* 1889.

On his return from Africa in 1903, Baden-Powell found that his military manual *Aids to Scouting* had become a best seller. It was intended to help to train young soldiers but other boys liked the interesting and exciting things in it too. Soon groups of boys were meeting together and practicing some of the new Scouting ideas. They called themselves Boy Scouts. This surprised and pleased Lord Baden-Powell so much that he decided to rewrite the book specially for boys, but first he wanted to try out some of his ideas. To do this, he arranged an experimental camp, and in 1907 took just twenty four boys to Brownsea Island.

In those days people didn't go camping or caravanning as they do today, so this was something new and exciting. The boys were a mixed group – some came from factories, some from public schools, and some from the Boys' Brigade but they got on splendidly and had a wonderful time. They cooked on open fires, slept in tents and went swimming and hiking. They learnt how to track in open countryside, played exciting stalking and outdoor games and in the evenings they sat round a glowing camp fire while Baden-Powell told them 'ripping yarns' about his adventures.

When the camp was over, Baden-Powell finished his book *Scouting For Boys* and in 1908 it was published in six instalments, not with the idea of forming a new Youth Movement but merely to offer fresh ideas to existing leaders of young people. It fired the imagination of boys everywhere. They read the book, formed themselves into patrols, put on hats and scarves and shorts like the boy in the drawings on the front covers and called themselves Boy Scouts. *Scouting For Boys* has sold approximately 150 million copies and was the fourth bestselling book of the 20th century.

It was the boys themselves that started the Movement, and it all happened so fast and with such enormous enthusiasm that Baden-Powell just had to organise things. Within two years it had spread right round the world.

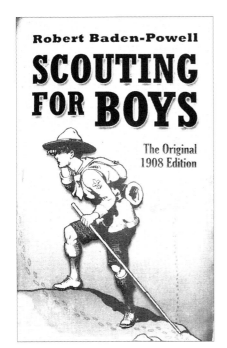

Part III. FORTNIGHTLY. Price 4d. net.

SCOUTING FOR BOYS BY B-P

(LIEUT. GEN. BADEN POWELL C.B.)

Part IV. FORTNIGHTLY. Price 4d. net.

SCOUTING FOR BOYS BY B-P

(LIEUT. GEN. BADEN POWELL C.B.)

Part V. FORTNIGHTLY. Price 4d. net.

SCOUTING FOR BOYS BY B-P

Part VI. Price 4d. net.

SCOUTING FOR BOYS BY B-P

(LIEUT. GEN. BADEN POWELL C.B.)

GIRLS WANTED TO BE IN
ON THE ACTION TOO

The perusal of *Scouting for Boys* however was not confined exclusively for boys, their sisters read the book which opened up new and appealing vistas to these Edwardian young ladies. All over the country groups of girls got together and called themselves Girl Scouts. This caused rather a problem for Baden-Powell who had envisaged Scouting as a male only thing, so when girls showed an interest, he was at a loss as to what to do. Even in the decorous Edwardian days when heavy chaperoning until marriage was the norm, young women were looking for fresh fields to conquer and barriers to break down. This was the age when women like Mrs Pankhurst and the suffragettes were trying to get women's emancipation, but it would be many more years before women could vote.

Single-sex education meant that girls were not allowed into university until Girton College for Women was founded at Hitchin in 1869 then transferred to Cambridge in 1873. Oxford followed this example several years later, and although this was an important point in the development of women's education it aroused scandalised protests from many quarters.

Understandably BP was opposed to the idea of a co-educational Scout group; the very idea would have shocked Edwardian society. But the girls had other ideas. When the Scouts held their first big Rally at Crystal Palace on September 4th 1909, the girls turned up and demanded to be included. The girls not only wanted to be Scouts, they meant to be.

By November 1909, 6,000 girls had registered as Girl Scouts at the new Scout Headquarters in London, using only their initials so that no one would recognise that they were girls, and there were many hundreds more all over the country not registered.

At the beginning of the 20th century, girls were expected to stay at home and learn such useful, but ordinary things as hemming and mending sheets and curtains, cleaning and cooking daily meals. They were only allowed to go for walks, provided that they did so in a ladylike manner. The idea of allowing and even encouraging girls to join in outdoor activities was frowned upon and any girl acting like a boy was called a tom-boy or a hoyden.

'If a girl is not allowed to run or even hurry, to swim, ride a bike, or raise her arms above her head, how can she become a Scout?' asked one enquiry that was printed in the *Scout Headquarters Gazette* 1909.

In 1910 Lieutenant-General Baden-Powell decided to retire from the army, believing that he could better serve his country by promoting scouting, and undaunted by public opinion, he decided to organise a sister movement.

Instead of being called Girl Scouts, he changed their name to Girl Guides, being inspired to name them after the famous corps of Guides in India who were then well known for their keen-ness, courage and general devotion to duty. They were the ones who led the way on difficult and dangerous expeditions.

Baden Powell published his ideas for the new organisation in the *Scout Headquarters Gazette*. His pamphlets A and B – *Baden-Powell Girl Guides, a Suggestion for Character Training For Girls* were re-works of *Scouting for Boys*, and the precursors to the *Guide Handbook*. The girls were thrilled but many parents were outraged. The ideas behind this new organisation for girls proved too much for some observers, and critics denounced the idea as a mischievous new development that would encourage girls to be unwomanly. They called it a foolish and pernicious movement.

Undaunted, the first Companies were started in 1910. The uniform of the Girl Guides was a navy blue blouse and a navy blue skirt that scarcely reached their ankles. Originally they retained the wide brimmed khaki scout hats although smaller ones were also introduced. Each guide wore a white haversack over one shoulder and on the haversack was a big red cross. These haversacks were filled with first aid items – bandages, slings, splints and safety pins. Like the Scouts, each Guide also carried a pole intended to be used to vault over streams, make a stretcher or hold back crowds from an accident.

Baden-Powell roped in his younger sister Agnes (Azzie) Smyth Baden-Powell born on December 16th 1858. Agnes had many varied interests and talents. She was an artist and accomplished musician, playing the organ, piano and violin. She was skilled in many of the homecrafts and handicrafts of the day and a member of the Queen Mary's Needlework Guild.

She was interested in natural history and astronomy. In her London home she had birds flying freely and a colony of live butterflies. She also kept bees in a glass hive. There was a hole in the hive fitted with a pipe which passed through a hole in the wall to outside. By passing along this pipe, the worker bees made their way to and from the nearby park. The honey they produced won prizes.

She was an adventurer and with her younger brother Baden she helped make silk hot air balloons and as an early balloonist made many flights. Later she helped with aeroplane building and in 1938 was an honorary companion of the Royal Aeronautical Society. She was involved in the Red Cross and the League of Mercy.

What better person to help Baden-Powell launch the new Girl Guide Movement! Agnes Baden-Powell's character, her gentle influence and love of all womanly arts were just the qualities needed to counteract the popular opinion that Guiding would make girls immodest, impolite tom-boys. She set a perfect example showing that girls joining the movement could combine the more traditional home-making skills such as sewing and cooking with exciting outdoor pursuits. It was thanks to her personality and enthusiasm that popular opinion was swayed and the movement gained many supporters.

The Handbook which BP wrote jointly with Agnes was called *How Girls Can Help To Build Up the Empire* and was published in 1912, the same year that Agnes brought about the formation of the 1st Lone Company.

War was declared on Germany on August 5th 1914 and Lord Kitchener was appointed Secretary of State for war. He immediately called for 100,000 volunteers for three years or the duration of the war. That number was set because equipment was so limited it was almost impossible to provide enough for even that number.

It was the enormous demands made by the fighting services on the nations man-power that provided both an opportunity and a challenge to the women of Britain. The urgency of the demand overcame prejudice and thousands of women volunteered to fill men's jobs in offices and factories, on the land, in transportation, postwomen and in munitions work of all kinds. Without their efforts, the armies could not have been maintained in men or materials. As a result it became widely accepted that woman had earned some of the rights hitherto reserved to men.

This was recognised when in 1915 the Girl Guide Movement was given official recognition and Agnes was made President at the same time. But to take the lead roll in this new and exciting organisation needed energy and drive, and Agnes was already in her fifties and a spinster caring for an elderly mother. She resigned from the Presidency in favour of Princess Mary in 1917, but continued in her role as Vice-President until her death in June 1945 at the age of 86.

Agnes Baden-Powell had done much to change public opinion about the role of girls and women, and the first world war gave woman a freedom and resilience that had never been known before, enabling the Girl Guide Movement to develop to the full.

THE GUIDE AND SCOUT BADGES

The Scout and Guide badges have been worn by millions and are the most widely recognised emblems in the world.

The basic arrowhead design of the Scout badge is usually associated with direction. As Lady Baden-Powell said, '*It shows the true way to go.*' But pointing is only one aspect of the arrowhead design trefoil. It has often been used in the coat of arms of many old, wealthy families. Sometimes the design was intended to represent a lance or spear, a lily – the fleur de lys, and even a bee or toad. The arrowhead selected by scouting's founder points the way to service and unity for scouts.

The Guide badge is a trefoil. The three leaves represent the three fold promise as laid down by the founder. The vein in the centre is the compass needle pointing the way and the stalk at the bottom is a heraldic fey or fire, standing for the love of mankind. The gold colour represents the shining sun.

OLAVE DEVOTES HERSELF
TO A LIFETIME OF GUIDING

In 1914 when World War I was declared, Girl Guides and Girl Scouts offered their services as volunteers in many countries including the United Kingdom, Austria and Poland. New groups emerged in France, Switzerland, Belgium, Czechoslovakia and Luxembourg. Guides acted as messengers for Marconi wireless telegraphs and were eligible for the War Service Badge. Olave offered her services to the Girl Guide Association but was turned down by Agnes and her committee as being too young, but undeterred, she wrote her first message in the *Girl Guide Gazette*.

BP put himself at the disposal of the War Office, but no command was given him. It was widely rumoured that he was engaged in spying and intelligence officers took great care to inculcate the myth. During his visits to France he had been impressed by the work of the Y.M.C.A. in providing recreational huts where the troops could relax, but the number of huts was woefully inadequate. Through his contacts, BP managed to provide a hut sponsored by the Mercers' Company at Val-de-Lievres, Calais to be staffed by men and women connected with scouting.

By 1915, Olave was feeling frustrated that she was not doing more for the war effort and four months after giving birth to Heather Grace on June 1st 1915, she set off for France to spend three months at Val-de-Lievres.

With scant knowledge but great enthusiasm, she was encouraged to plunge in, and the hitherto undiscovered qualities of resourcefulness and stoicism of this privileged young lady began to show through. She was undaunted by the discomforts of life in wartime France, and not content with being just a figure head, she worked long hours dispensing chat and sympathy along with cocoa and cigarettes to the war weary men.

The first world war did not stop the progression of the Guide/Scout movement and Olave's involvement had a profound influence upon the Association. She worked throughout the war years to build up the Girl Guide organization, endlessly recruiting leaders and commissioners. In March 1916 Olave was granted a warrant as County Commissioner for Sussex and in October appointed Chief Commissioner. She published a pamphlet called *The Girl Guide Movement* and the following year published *Training Girls as Guides*.

The arrival of daughter Betty in 1917 completed the family, but even with three young children to raise, Olave always found time to accompany BP to the many functions and rallies he attended. Wherever they went they had the kind of reception that is given

nowadays to pop-stars and footballers.

In 1918 Olave was acclaimed Chief Guide at the County Commissioners' Conference and presented with 'Silver Fish' the highest Guide Award. In Olave's case, the silver fish was gold as a

token of the Commissioners' esteem.

Working alongside her husband to achieve a common goal, awakened in Olave qualities and talents she had no idea she possessed. They were leading brother and sister movements and each ran their own show while happily contributing to the other's work.

Olave and B.P. toured extensively and were welcomed everywhere with great enthusiasm by the thousands of young people who were

84

flocking to join the world brotherhood and sisterhood of Scouts and Guides. Olave admitted that it was thrilling but exhausting. '*I could have filled all my days and nights as well with Guiding affairs, but my days were also filled with the multitude of small, mundane details that go into the bringing up of a family and running a home,*' she said.

From 1919-39, they lived at Pax Hill near Bentley, Hampshire, a gift from her father who had died in 1918. In 1919 when Betty was just two, and four months after moving to Pax Hill, Olave's elder sister Auriol suddenly died, leaving three small daughters aged seven, six and eighteen months, and a tea planter husband in Ceylon. Without hesitation Olave and her husband took these girls into their family, instantly doubling its size. As a mother of six and wife of a retired General, Olave had staff to help run the household, but each week she typed out a programme showing what was happening each day. There was a copy for the cook, chauffer and housemaids. It listed what train her husband would travel to London, which car she would want ready to drive herself, when to take the children to classes, who was coming to stay and for how many nights, which bedrooms were to be made ready, who and how many for dinner each day – all times and details precisely given.

There was always a mass of mail to reply to and right up into later life, Olave sent out over 2,000 Christmas cards to her first name friends. Many of the early ones were hand painted by BP.

AN INDIVIDUALLY PAINTED GREETINGS CARD BY BP

At the 5th International Conference in Hungary in 1928, delegates from 26 countries finally decided that the World Association of Girl Guides and Girl Scouts should be established with a World Bureau

OUT OF UNIFORM BUT STILL WEARING THEIR SCOUT AND GUIDE BADGES

in London as its secretariat. In 1929 and 1930, Egypt and Greece joined and the movement spread through Africa, Asia and America.

In 1929, B.P. was created Baron Baden-Powell and their three children automatically took the courtesy title of The Honourable.

When Olave was presented with her own Guide Standard and accepted the position of World Chief Guide in 1930, a post she held for the rest of her life, she promised to do her best, to offer the hand of friendship around the world. By this time membership was over one million, and Olave had became affectionately known as the 'mother of millions'.

A RETURN VISIT TO CHESTERFIELD

The new headquarters of the Chesterfield Division of the Girl Guide Association was opened by Lady Baden Powell on May 16th 1930 in the presence of a large and distinguished gathering.

The building, situated between St Margaret's Drive and Cross Street was made possible because of the generosity of Mr A.A. Townrow and Mr C. J. Howson who gave the land for the new hall, the Chesterfield architect Mr Derbyshire for his artistic design, and the builders Mr Chas. Vallance and Son, Mansfield. The hall has a seating capacity of 300-350, an excellent stage, a library and kitchen facilities and cost £3,700.

On the arrival of the Chief Guide there was the breaking of the Colours, the salute and the reading of dedicatory prayers by the Archdeacon of Chesterfield, the Rev G. H. Clayton.

THE ARRIVAL OF THE CHIEF GUIDE

LADY BADEN-POWELL OFFICIALLY OPENED THE DOORS WITH A GOLDEN KEY

Lady Baden-Powell then formerly opened the main door with a golden key which was afterwards presented to her by the division. In performing the ceremony, she expressed the hope that the hall would help the Guides in all their work, that good would go on in its walls and that nothing but good would come out of it.

POSING FOR THE OFFICIAL PHOTOGRAPH

The Chairman at the outset extended a hearty greeting to their Chief Guide. She said they looked upon her as their own property, and she thought Chesterfield was owed a great debt of gratitude for giving Lady Baden-Powell to the world. She had accomplished a very wonderful feat, having started a marvellous organisation in almost every country in the world, thus making it possible for women of all kinds to come together in one big system.

In her speech, Lady Baden-Powell said how tremendously

proud, delighted and honoured she felt at being invited to be with them on such an important and great occasion in the history of Guiding in Chesterfield. She felt overcome when she realised that there in her birthplace, she would have the opportunity of being with her Guides and the townspeople of Chesterfield who had done so much for the movement.

She said how she loved her birthplace, and it was a tremendous privilege to come there and to learn a lesson – because she felt the erection of that building had been a very great lesson to many of them.

When she heard that the undertaking was being started, and that they in Chesterfield were going to launch out, take their courage in both hands and build that beautiful place, she thought they were setting a wonderful example. It was a very big undertaking to put into bricks and mortar so much of the world's good, and erect such a beautiful building, and it had shown that where there's a will there's a way and Guides would, when put to it make very great efforts.

Lady Baden Powell said it also showed what kind hearted supporters the movement had in Chesterfield, but there was a long way to go before they completed the fund for purchasing the building. However they were, she said more than half way there because possession was nine points of the law. This was met by laughter.

THE ONLY SURVIVING CUP AND SAUCER FROM 1930, SPECIALLY MADE FOR THE OPENING OF THE CHESTERFIELD GUIDE HEADQUARTERS

Not only was it a sign of tremendous pluck, to launch Guiding that way, she continued, but it was a sign of great strength of the movement in their midst. The Guide movement was a great strength in the country for good.

She reminded her audience that the idea of Scouting was started in 1907, the Guide movement was a great strength, and came along as a natural sequence. Something was needed to fill the gap between the teaching in the schools, the home and the churches, so the Scouting movement was started for boys and the Guides for girls to supplement the efforts of others in the training of the rising generation. The organization had grown from strength to strength until there were 2,000,000 Scouts and 1,000,000 Guides.

In promoting that character training, training in handicraft, health and citizenship amongst the children of Chesterfield, they were building better than they knew. The Guide law – a Guide smiles and sings under all difficulties, had been called nonsense by some people, but Lady Baden-Powell emphasised that having to put on a smile to overcome a difficulty, gave a certain strength and a stiffening to one's moral character.

The Duchess of Devonshire in seconding the vote of thanks to Lady Baden-Powell, said she felt it a great privilege to be there that day to see the wonderful function. She said it must be a source of great pleasure to Lady Baden-Powell to see the result of her involvement with the movement take a tangible form, and the great energy and life in the movement in her native town. It was some reward to Lady Baden-Powell for the marvellous work she had done, and it was wonderful that Lady Baden-Powell had allowed a wreath of Olives to be woven into the Guide's standard to indicate her special connection with the Guide Movement in Chesterfield.

THE CHESTERFIELD GUIDE STANDARD SHOWING THE TREFOIL BADGE, THE COUNTY BADGE, THE POMEGRANATE WHICH IS IN THE CHESTERFIELD COAT OF ARMS (SEE WALK), THE GUIDE MOTTO AND THE SPECIAL WREATH OF OLIVES THAT OLAVE, LADY BADEN POWELL ALLOWED TO BE WOVEN INTO THE DESIGN TO INDICATE HER SPECIAL CONNECTION WITH THE GUIDE MOVEMENT IN CHESTERFIELD

A SPECIAL GIFT FOR CHESTERFIELD

On June 19ᵗʰ 1938. Olave wrote from Pax Hill, Bentley, Hampshire –
    'I have this week sent off a picture to Chesterfield which I offer with affection and good wishes to the Guide headquarters of that Division.
    This portrait was done by Mr H.H.J. Baird in 1904, when I was Guide age, and I felt that I would like it now to belong to my birthplace, if your Guides there would like to accept it.
    I little thought at the time when that picture was painted, what I should

eventually be called upon to do in my life. I played about care free and content with my ponies and my precious spaniel, never dreaming what responsibility was to rest on my shoulders when I emerged from that happy childhood spent at that time in Devonshire.

I hope that the picture may hang on the walls of your beautiful Guide Hall and be a silent witness of many happy and delightful Guide doings there.

Olave was fifteen, 5ft 4ins and weighed 6 stone 8lbs when she had this portrait painted. The following year she was so excited when she saw it on display in a London gallery. Her canine companion is Doogy her beloved spaniel who in her letter is referred to as 'my precious spaniel'. Doogy went with her everywhere and one year at Harvest Thanksgiving trotted up the aisle in the middle of the sermon, right up to the chancel where Olave was sitting in the choir. The following year he became ill with mange and despite her tender nursing, died on April 10th 1907. In her diary Olave wrote –

' The most miserable day in my life. Rained. The sky and I weep in unison. Doogy the Divine, my own darling and precious dog had to be shot.'

Many years later Olave said she wept for him for three whole days and it was a long time before she could speak of him dryeyed. Even a year later, if she was sad, she would howl at the remembrance of her darling dog.

THE MOTHER OF MILLIONS

For a woman who has so many memorable milestones in her life it is hard to select just a few.

In the birthday honours list of 1932, Olave was awarded a GBE, and made a Dame Grand Cross of the British Empire for her self-less devotion to the Girl Guide Association. She attended the Guides 21st birthday service, which she referred to as the 'Coming of Age' year for guiding, held in St Paul's Cathedral, London, where a congregation of 5,300 guides renewed their promise.

Olave's mother, Katharine Soames died in 1932 and the years were taking their toll on BP.

Having made her first radio broadcast in 1923, in 1938, Olave made her first television broadcast from Alexandra Palace. In the same year, she and BP who was in his 80th year left Britain in live in Kenya.

They were in Nyeri, Kenya where BP had previously been to recuperate when war was declared in September 1939. His ill health and the war prevented their return to England. The little cottage where they lived was named Paxtu and was located in the grounds of the Outspan Hotel.

They had been together for 27 years when BP died on January 8th 1941. Lt. Gen Sir Robert Baden-Powell 1st Lord Baden-Powell of Gilwell, Essex, GCB, GCMG, GCVO, OM was laid to rest in St Peter's Cemetery in Nyeri.

Olave managed to return to London in 1942 but felt alone, depressed and homeless. Pax Hill was occupied by Canadian troops, even if she could have afforded to go back there. Money was a problem so she moved into the international scout office, sleeping on a camp bed with her few possessions in a suitcase for almost four months until she was given a Grace and Favour Apartment at Hampton Court Palace where she spent the next thirty one years.

Olave gave Pax Hill to the Girl Guide Association to be used as a Guide Homecraft Training Centre. It was sold in 1953. The Paxtu cottage in Kenya was integrated into the Outspan Hotel building and serves as a small Scouting museum.

THE CHATSWORTH JUBILEE CAMP

To celebrate fifty years of Guiding, three generations of Scouting's famous Baden-Powell family were at Derbyshire's Jubilee Camp held in Chatsworth Park in June 1960, and heading the distinguished guests was seventy one year old Lady Baden-Powell, World Chief Guide.

To celebrate this Jubilee camp, the Derbyshire Girl Guide Association produced three issues of 'The Chatsworth Highway' a double page camp newspaper, and on the front page of the first issue was a letter from The Chief Guide. The message still holds strong, fifty years later.

Hullo Guides!
As I sit writing this message for you on a wet day in April, camp still seems rather a long time ahead, but the looking forward is all part of the fun and I am looking forward to being with you in June just as you will have been looking forward to this camp for a long time.

And when it is all over it will be something for us all to look back on with – I am sure – happiness for a long time.

It is like that with the whole of Guiding. In this Jubilee Year, some of us older ones will be looking back quite a long way, and rejoicing in all that our movement has achieved, and all that it has meant to us, in the first fifty years of its existence.

You can't exactly do that! But you can look forward to the next fifty years and to the time when you who are guides in Jubilee Year will be the Guiders and Leaders of the Movement, and so putting back into Guiding some of the good things and the fun which it has given to you.

So whether you look backwards or forwards or both, let us join in celebrating our Jubilee Year with happiness and thankfulness for the great game given to us by our founder fifty years ago.

BEST WISHES for "GOOD CAMPING" and "GOOD GUIDING" to you all!

As she wrote in her letter, she was looking forward to the camp and on June 6ᵗʰ 1960, there was an air of great excitement as 1,600 Guides waited for her arrival. At 10.15 a.m on that Monday

DERBYSHIRE GIRL GUIDE ASSOCIATION

THE
CHATSWORTH
HIGHWAY

| JUBILEE CAMP ISSUE No. ONE | PRICE 3d. | SATURDAY JUNE 4th, 1960 |

Hullo Guides !

A S I sit writing this message for you on a wet day in April, camp still seems rather a long time ahead, but the looking forward is all part of the fun and I am looking forward to being with you in June just as you will have been looking forward to this camp for a long time.

And when it is all over it will be something for us all to look back on with—I am sure—happiness for a long time.

It is like that with the whole of Guiding. In this Jubilee Year some of us older ones will be looking back quite a long way, and rejoicing in all that our Movement has achieved, and all that it has meant to us, in the first fifty years of its existence.

You can't exactly do that ! But you can look forward to the next fifty years and to the time when you who are Guides in Jubilee Year will be the guiders and leaders of the Movement, and so putting back into guiding some of the good things and the fun which it has given to you.

So, whether we look backwards or forwards or both, let us join in celebrating our Jubilee Year with happiness and thankfulness for the great game given to us by our Founder fifty years ago.

BEST WISHES for "GOOD CAMPING" and "GOOD GUIDING" to you all !

Of our Baden-Powell
Chief Guide

Welcome to all Campers at the Derbyshire Jubilee Camp at Chatsworth !

A S we enjoy our days in camp in this lovely park we will think of all the other Rangers and Guides who are also in camp at this time or celebrating the Jubilee in different ways. We will think too of all those who have camped during the past fifty years from whom we have learned so much—those pioneers who have taught us how to make ourselves comfortable in a tent and how to enjoy living out-of-doors.

I would like to give a special welcome to our visitors from Overseas who are sharing this week-end with us—we are delighted to have them and I am sure we shall learn a lot from each other.

We are looking forward to seeing the Chief Guide on Monday and I know that you will give her a great welcome. We are very lucky that she is able to be with us for a whole day at this very busy time.

May this Jubilee Camp provide a store of happy memories for us all

Betty McInnes,
Assistant County Commissioner.

The visitors to the Camp will include (in addition to Lady Baden-Powell) Miss C. E. Patteson (Camp Adviser, Commonwealth H.Q.) Mrs. J. A. Common (Camp Adviser for England), Miss W. Simmons (Midland Area Camp Adviser) Sir Ian Walker Okeover (Lord Lieutenant for Derbyshire) and Lady Walker-Okeover (County President of the Guides)

The picture (above) shows Miss Patteson chatting with Guides from overseas at the Windsor World Camp in 1957.

morning the Chief Guide arrived, escorted by her daughter The Hon. Mrs Betty Clay, Guide Commissioner in Northern Rhodesia and her husband Mr Gervas Clay, Provincial Commissioner there. Their son Robin Clay, Lady Baden-Powell's grandson was also there and many years later explained that she was at all times aware of the intense planning and preparation that went into

1910-B.P.-1960

_____ *of the*

_____ *Company*

attended/visited the

Derbyshire Jubilee Camp

Chatsworth Park

June 1960

as shown by this seal

LEFT: THE JUBILEE CAKE WAS MADE UP OF BOXES CONTAINING ONE SEAL FOR EACH GUIDE ATTENDING.
RIGHT: THE OFFICIAL CERTIFICATE OF DERBYSHIRE JUBILEE CAMP WITH THE OFFICIAL SEAL IN THE RIGHT BOTTOM CORNER

organizing an event, and the great air of expectancy as the time for her visit approached, so she always made sure that she arrived spot on time. This usually meant that in order to arrive punctually she actually arrived quite some time before the 'official' time. Having sent a message to the organizers to say that she was there, she would then wait round the corner, so that her official arrival was timed to perfection.

After the colour ceremonial, Lady Baden-Powell gave a short speech then representatives from each division went forward to collect 'slices' of what appeared to be a huge, iced birthday cake.

The cake was in fact made up of boxes containing Jubilee seals, enough for every Guide in the camp.

Lady Baden-Powell presented awards and toured the camp in an open Land Rover before going to Chatsworth House for lunch.

She returned in the afternoon to watch the Scout pageant, a re-enactment of the

LADY BADEN-POWELL TOURED THE CAMP IN AN OPEN LAND ROVER

life of the founder. Lady

Baden-Powell watched her son, Lord Peter Baden-Powell and her teenage grandson, the Hon. Michael Baden-Powell play BP as a man and a boy.

That evening at 7.30, Lady Baden-Powell lit a burning torch then lit the torch of a Guide and together they lit the camp fire. Camp fire songs, and stunts followed. As well as the old favourites like All Night, All Day; Rock O' My Soul; Kum Ba Yah, there was also the Jubilee Song, and each division was asked to make up a verse for a special Chatsworth Camp Song.

I am extremely grateful to Mr Robin Clay who has rooted out his mother's diary for that day and has allowed us to use it.

Monday Felted 10-ish & went to Chatsworth Park, home of Duke & Duchess of Devonshire, for Derbyshire County Camp, & Scout Camp & Rally – a really BIG day. On arrival at the central place the guides were all gathered to make an avenue between the flags of all the countries & we walked up this avenue behind Mum, with the Duke & [crossed out] the Chief Scout Sir Charles Maclean, the Lord Lieut & wife, & Robin who appeared from the Scout Camp, & the Guides cheered & waved in wildest excitement – Speeches, presentation of Awards, from a Land Rover, speaking through a Megaphone-type of microphone, rather hampering. Then Coffee with the Guiders & then Mum went round the camps, in the L.R. & stopped at each one for a few minutes. So G. & Robin & I went round too, to different ones, walking. They had all made smart gateways, depicting "milestones" of Guiding: 1910, Brownies called Rosebuds, World Assn started, Foxlease, etc. & two were the traditional Well-Dressing done for festivals in this county. Then we went to Chatsworth House for grand lunch in huge lovely dining room, the apartments newly done-up & they have only lived here a few months. The rest of the house

The transcription of The Hon. Mrs Clay's diary reads –

Monday June –

Fetched tenish and went to Chatsworth Park, home of the Duke and Duchess of Devonshire, for Derbyshire County Camp and Scout Camp and Rally – a really big day. On arrival at the central place, the guides were all gathered to make an avenue between the flags of all the countries and we walked up this avenue behind Mum with the Duke and Duchess, the Chief Scout, Sir Charles MacLean, the Lord Lieutenant and wife, and Robin who appeared from the Scout Camp. The guides cheered and waved in wildest excitement. Speeches, presentation of awards from a Land Rover speaking through a megaphone-type of microphone – neither hampering.

Then coffee with the guides and then Mum went around the camps in the L.R. and stopped at each one for a few minutes. So G and Robin and I went around too, to different ones walking.

They had all made smart gateways depicting 'milestones' of Guiding: 1910 Brownies called Rosebuds; World Association started, Foxlease etc. and two were the traditional Well-Dressing done for festivals in this county.

Then we went to Chatsworth House for grand lunch in huge, lovely dining room, the apartments newly done up, and they have only lived here a few months. The rest of the house is open to the public to try to make money to keep it up. 2/6 (12½ p) a head and 7,000 came in yesterday, the peak day of the year.

Robert and Mike, both neat and sensible and well-behaved.

Lunch was 'help yourself' with wonderful food and beautiful silver etc.

Then we all drove to the Scout Rally, and walked right across a great arena to a row of chairs along the huge crowd on the hillside and there we watched the Cubs give the Chief Scout a Grand Howl. Then the Scouts did the Pageant of Dad's life, which they did at the Jamboree. Very well done with a huge cast and first rate stage management of scenery and props. Peter and another man alternated to act Dad so no delay between one scene and another. After Peter had walked away and disappeared, Robert read his last message – very well indeed.

Then there was rather an anti-climax in the presenting of

101

Queen's Scout Awards which took ages, and then…Very difficult to get away in the cars all parked head to tail on grass in milling crowds. What a crowd – dozens of buses and hundreds of cars.

Back to the Guide Camp where we had tea. Then we actually sat quietly and peacefully in the Guide H.Q. They gave us supper then camp fire up on the high slope above the camp with wonderful view over Derbyshire hills. Quite good singing led by Brin, and Mum spoke. They were a most responsive lot, prepared to answer anything and to laugh and clap and cheer at any moment. Then she called on me to speak too and they were just as enthusiastic. Afterwards 3 came specially to give me messages to my Guides and two gave little camp badges to give to them.

As we walked down through the camp, little groups of them cheered again and again. I've never known Guides so ready to cheer at anything and anybody.

Then drove home, coffee and fell into bed.

At the close of Guiding events, a special hymn called Taps is sung. The name comes from the American army where the tapping on a drum was used as a signal, later replaced by a bugle call, to tell the men that it was time to retire for the night.

I was fortunate to be at the Jubilee camp in 1960 and as we sat round the dying embers of a giant campfire in Chatsworth Park on that final evening, Lady Baden-Powell made her goodnight speech. I don't remember the words but I do remember, she pointed to the west where the most amazing sunset was colouring the night sky. Every guide turned to look as we sang Taps. It was an experience few who were there will ever forget.

DAY IS DONE
GONE THE SUN
FROM THE SEA
FROM THE HILLS
FROM THE SKY
ALL IS WELL
SAFELY REST
GOD IS NIGH

THE FINAL CHAPTER

For nearly sixty years, Lady Baden-Powell travelled the world spreading the word, and devoting her life to Guiding. But she wasn't just a figurehead, she was a great friend to many and enjoyed a wicked sense of humour.

While staying at Waddow, the Guide Training Centre, she slipped and fell down the stairs breaking six ribs. The secretary rushed out of the office and exclaimed – 'Oh thank goodness it's only you. I was afraid it was the new Hoover.'

In 1969 on her eightieth birthday she read the lesson at the Thinking Day Service in Westminster Abbey. 1970 was the Guide Diamond Jubilee Year and she travelled extensively until in July it was discovered that she was suffering from diabetes. Her failing heath caused her to give up long-distance travel, but by this time she had travelled 487,000 miles by air, not counting travel by sea, road and rail. She had travelled around the world five times, making more than 650 flights and visiting 111 countries to promote Scouting and Guiding worldwide.

It was only when she was eighty with failing health that she professed herself to be in semi-retirement. She continued her work at home and the accolades kept coming.

In 1972, Harry Wheatcroft often referred to as 'Mr Rose' named

a red tea rose after her. He arrived at Guide Head Quarters with a most exciting looking oblong box tucked under his arm, and as it was unpacked, between layers of tissue paper, out came masses of the most glorious fragrant scarlet roses. Immediately, an armful were rushed round to Hampton Court Palace where the Chief Guide received them with delight. Lady Baden Powell had given her blessing to her name-sake and that first year, 10,000 bushes were sold.

Olave Baden-Powell

In 1974 she was the subject on the Ceres medal produced each year by the Food and Agriculture organization.

She had led a life of great fulfilment. Her contribution to the movement was enormous, her humour and compassion remembered by all those with whom she came into contact. But her greatest legacy is the continued world-wide success of a movement that she did so much to shape.

In 1973 her autobiography *Window on My Heart* was published and in it was this letter.

In 1973, she moved from Hampton Court to Birtley House, a nursing home near Guildford where she passed away on June 25th 1977 aged 88. The funeral service took place privately on July 1st in the little church in Bentley and her ashes were taken to Kenya where they were ceremoniously placed in the grave of her beloved husband.

My dear Guides,

And I include Rangers and Brownies and Guiders and all of you, and the Scout people too— everyone in fact who is bound by the Promise and Law of our Movement.

There was a time when I could have spoken to each one of you individually and given you a left-handshake—as I do to a great many of you every week—but as our family now numbers not hundreds of thousands but millions, and is so widely scattered about the world, I just can't get round to you all.

So here is the next best thing— a book through which I hope you will not only get to know me more as a person, but also will get to know what I think and feel about you, and how deeply I care for every single one of you, whoever and wherever you may be.

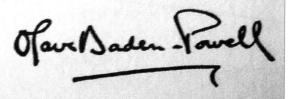

Their joint headstone is engraved with a small circle, a dot in its centre, the Guide/Scout tracking sign for 'Gone Home'.

On September 26th 1977, a Thanksgiving Service for Olave was held in Westminster Abbey, and on February 12th 1981, joint memorial stones were dedicated to Olave and Robert Baden-Powell. This was the first joint memorial in the Abbey.

THEIR JOINT HEADSTONE IS ENGRAVED WITH A SMALL CIRCLE, A DOT IN ITS CENTRE, THE GUIDE/SCOUT TRACKING SIGN FOR 'GONE HOME'

OLAVE, LADY BADEN-POWELL'S LAST MESSAGE

Dear Guides, Scouts, Cubs and Brownies and all their leaders and friends

I shall have left this world when you receive this message, which I leave to express my thanks for all the kindness and the affection shown to me, and to say how greatly I have rejoiced over the way in which you have all carried out your share in the work of the movement that my beloved husband invented, for the advancement of the boys and girls of all countries, years ago.

I have firm belief in Almighty God and in the life in the world to come, when he and I will be re-united; and together we shall watch over you who have been enrolled as members of this world family, and go on caring for your progress and your well-being.

I trust that you will continue fully to use the system of work and play that our movement provides, keeping up the fun and the friendships made at our meetings and in camps, abiding by the Promise and up-holding the Laws that you undertook to live by when you joined up.

In that way, you will not only advance yourself in body, mind and spirit, but you will affect those around you, and in doing what is honourable and right and wise, and in giving out kindness of thought and action, thus striving against all ills and helping to make the world a happier and a better place to live.

I trust that you will be successful in all your tasks, and may God be with you in the coming years.

WORLD THINKING DAY

It must be quite unusual for a husband and wife to share the same day and month of birth, but not amongst the Baden Powells. Not only did BP and Olave share a birthday, their son Peter shared his birthday with his wife, and their younger daughter Betty shared her birthday with her eldest son and with her husband whom she had met on board ship, as her parents had met. And the second son of their elder daughter Heather was born also on his grandparent's joint birthday.

In 1927 it was decided to have a special day in the Guide/Scout year that could be celebrated annually, and what better day than February 22ⁿᵈ, the birthdate of both Lord and Lady Baden-Powell. Olave is quoted as saying *'The conference paid Robin (her pet name for BP.) and me the compliment of choosing our joint birthday, February 22ⁿᵈ, as Thinking Day'*.

The Scouts call it Founders Day; the Guides call it Thinking Day and it is one of the most significant dates in the guiding calendar with ceremonies and celebrations taking place throughout the world.

Before dawn that day, Guides and Rangers in Auckland, New Zealand climb to the top of Mount Eden. There they set up a camp-fire and a flag-pole and as the sun rises above the horizon, they raise the Guide World Flag. They sing the World Song and they think about the founders and the family of guiding. They send Guiding Happy Birthday wishes and prayers to fellow members, thus promoting international friendship and understanding, and in so doing, they start the 'Big Think' which then travels all around the world.

Every year on Thinking Day Olave was always snowed under

with letters, messages, cables, telegrams, packages, parcels and greetings of every kind on Thinking Day. The greeting cards came from companies, troops and individuals. They were often hand made and beautifully designed. Messages from every corner of the world where Guiding existed arrived by the truck load, all written in beautiful English.

'Kind thoughts are certainly circling the earth today,' Lady Baden-Powell wrote, 'and we ourselves feel quite overwhelmed by the kindliness showered upon us in thought from afar and greetings from those around us. All that we can say is Thank You, Thank You, Thank You.'

In 1932 at The 7th World Conference in Poland, a delegate suggested that the girls' appreciation and friendship should not only be shown by the exchanging of wishes, but also through presents, which are after all typical of birthdays. This led to the practical suggestion that on Thinking Day, each Guide throughout the world should contribute *'A Penny For Your Thoughts'* towards the World Association Fund which is then used to help packs and companies all round the world.

Another tradition is for all Guides and ex-Guides to place a lit candle in their window at dusk, as in the Guiding song *'This Little Guiding Light of Mine, I'm going to let it shine.'*

In 1999 at the 30th World Conference in Ireland, it was decided to change the name Thinking Day to World Thinking Day in order to emphasise the global aspect of this special day. Amateur radio links were set up in many places to enable guides to talk on air. One of these was at Wingerworth to cater for the thousands of guides who wanted to send greetings to the guides at Olave's place of birth. With the internet revolution, World Thinking Day is now also promoted on Face book and Twitter.

The World Association of Girl Guides and Girl Scouts chooses a theme for each World Thinking Day and proposes related activities. The theme for 2011 is *'Empowering Girls Will Change Our World'*.

In London, World Thinking Day 2011 was celebrated with a special evensong service at Westminster Abbey led by John Hall, the Dean of Westminster. Dedicated to Girlguiding UK and The Scout Association, wreaths were laid at the memorials of Robert and Olave Baden-Powell.

One hundred and fifty miles away in Chesterfield an equally memorable service was being held, the unveiling of a Blue Plaque to Olave, Lady Baden-Powell, one hundred and twenty two years after her birth that day in February 22nd 1889.

Lady Baden-Powell blue plaque unveiling
Tuesday 22nd February 2011

1.30pm onwards:	You are invited to join the Mayor and Mayoress of Chesterfield for light refreshments in the Town Hall.
2pm:	Girlguiding UK members assemble in front of the Town Hall.
2.15pm:	Everyone makes their way to the plaque unveiling site in Shentall Gardens in front of the Town Hall.
2.30pm:	Welcome. Speech by Councillor Lewer and then the unveiling.
3.15pm:	Invitees to walk to Chesterfield Guides HQ for refreshments, light entertainment and presentations.
3.30pm:	Singing from Ashgate District. Teas and coffees by Trefoil Guild.
3.50pm:	Presentations.
4.15pm approx:	Close of event.

A BLUE PLAQUE TO HONOUR
LADY BADEN-POWELL

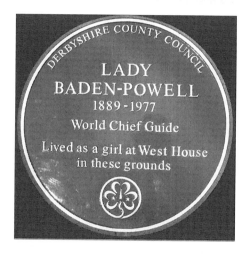

The Derbyshire Blue Plaque scheme was launched in 2009 when nominations were invited from the public covering themes such as war heroes, local heroes and famous people; cultural and heritage connections, philanthropists and entrepreneurs and buildings of historic and architectural importance.

From 63 nominations, a short list of 12 was drawn up from which the six winners were chosen by public vote.

'We received more than 25,000 votes and I would like to say a big thank you to everyone who took part,' said Councillor Andrew Lewer, Derbyshire County Council leader and cabinet member for culture. 'They are all worthy winners.'

The names of the first six people to be honoured in Derbyshire were revealed on July 10th 2010, and the clear favourite, with 72% of votes cast was Lady Baden-Powell, nominated for a plaque by Louise Collins of New Whittington, the runner-up was George Stephenson with just 5% of votes. Louise was ten when she became a guide and is now a Chesterfield Ranger and Brown Owl of 1st Holme Hall Brownies. She cited Lady Baden Powell as a major influence in her life.

Louise said *'Lady Baden-Powell was a truly inspirational forward thinking woman whose legacy continues today through a world-wide movement of 10 million women in 145 countries. I believe it empowers girls and young women and gives them the confidence to try new things and take on new challenges – its also about great friendships and having fun.*

It was pioneering for a woman to set up such a group as that time when these kinds of activities were not seen as suitable for girls, but there was a place for them then and with 50,000 girls currently on the waiting list, there's obviously still a place for it now. There are more than 10,000 members in Derbyshire and for Lady Baden Powell to be honoured in this way is especially brilliant in what is Girlguiding UK's centenary year.'

Crowds watched the Derbyshire County Council memorial unveiling by Holme Hall brownie, nine year old Hallie Baron, and council leader Clr. Andrew Lewer on Tuesday February 22nd 2011.

Glory for a guiding light

By Ellen Beardmore

"WHEN I say beloved, that's not just by her family but by ten million Guides all over the world".

Those moving words remembered inspirational Guiding chief Lady Olave Baden-Powell as she was honoured with a blue plaque in Chesterfield's Shentall Memorial Gardens on Rose Hill the site of her childhood home.

Crowds watched the Derbyshire County Council memorial unveiling by Holme Hall recruit Hallie Baron (9) and council leader Cllr Andrew Lewer, on Tuesday.

Treasured memories of Lady Baden-Powell, an unconventional, determined woman who never forgot a face, were also shared by a special guest, her grandson Robin Clay.

"When I say beloved, that's not just by her family but by ten million Guides all over the world", said an emotional Mr Clay (71).

"Thank you for this plaque – Derbyshire is rightly proud of Lady Baden-Powell as a daughter."

Lady Baden-Powell, the wife of Scout and Guide founder Lord Robert Baden-Powell, became Chief Guide for Britain in 1919.

She died in 1977 and was nominated for a plaque by Louise Collins, leader of 1st Holme Hall Brownies and Chesterfield Rangers, receiving more than 18,000 public votes. One of her achievements was recruiting 2,860 Guide commissioners in just 18 months. There is a leader shortage today.

Speaking afterwards Mr Clay added: "I hope this will spark more to come forward – that would be a living memorial to her work."

HONOURED AT HOME: Cllr Lewer and Hallie Baron (9) unveil the plaque to Lady Olave Baden-Powell. Photo by Rebecca Havercroft. SSP88521

Celebrating Derbyshire's cultural and historical heritage is the aim of the blue plaque scheme, which has already honoured former Chatsworth gardener Sir Joseph Paxton and will commemorate four more legends in its first round.

Cllr Lewer said he was proud to see Lady Baden-Powell commemorated in her home county, adding: "She was a pioneer in her time and ensured the Guiding movement is what it is today."

For more on local Guiding visit www.gfhguildingderbyshire.org.
ellen beardmore
@derbyshiretimes.co.uk

'Celebrating Derbyshire's Cultural and historical heritage is the aim of the blue plaque scheme,' said Clr Lewer. 'I am proud to see Lady Baden-Powell commemorated in her home county. She was a pioneer in her time and ensured the Guiding movement is what it is today.'

Mr Robin Clay, Lady Baden-Powell's grandson was a special guest who spoke about his grandmother, sharing treasured memories of an unconventional, determined woman who never forgot a face. He said, 'Thank you for this plaque – Derbyshire is rightly proud of Lady Baden-Powell as a daughter. When I say she was beloved, that's not just by her family, but by ten million guides throughout the world.'

Speaking afterwards, Mr Clay added: 'I hope this will spark more guides and guiders to come forward – that would be a living memorial to her work.'

114

'JAM ROLL', THE BADEN-POWELL'S ROLLS ROYCE IN CHESTERFIELD.
'JAM ROLL' TOOK OLAVE TO BUCKINGHAM PALACE TO RECEIVE HER G.B.E.

Another attraction at the unveiling was 'Jam Roll', a 20 horse-power Rolls Royce car, registration number OU 2938 given to the Baden-Powells in 1929 during the 3rd World Scout Jamboree at Arrowe Park, near Liverpool. The money to buy it was raised by every Scout contributing just one penny. BP named it Jam Roll, Jam for Jamboree and Roll after the maker Rolls Royce, and also because at that time, a tea-time treat at Lyon's Corner House tea-shop anywhere in the country was a 'Penny Jam Roll'. Olave referred to the occasion as *'Scoutings Coming of Age'*, but probably of more significance, it was at that gathering that BP was awarded a peerage.

It was Jam Roll that took Olave to Buckingham Palace on that day in 1932 to receive her G.B.E. from King George V. As Olave said at the time 'I was jam-rolled to the palace for the investiture'. Together with a trailer caravan known as Eccles, the combination was used by the Baden-Powells in their travels round Europe. Jam Roll was sold in 1945. It's been a taxi in Manchester, then passed into private ownership.

Loaned by its owner, Jam Roll was reunited with Eccles at Gilwell Park, national headquarters and training centre, for the 21st World Scout Jamboree in 2007, when it was resolved to purchase Jam Roll on behalf of scouting. Jam Roll is on display at Rolls Royce Trust Heritage Museum in Derby. A patronage scheme to raise money to buy and maintain it has been set up. For details go to www.bpjamroll.org

ONE HUNDRED YEARS AND STILL GOING STRONG

More than half the female population of England have been members of what is now the largest women's organisation in the world. Currently there are nearly ten million girls, young women and adults in 144 countries involved as Leaders, Rangers, Guides and Brownies.

Derbyshire's links with guiding go back to 1910 when the first company was formed here.

DERBYSHIRE'S FIRST GUIDES

The Scout and Guide Movements are the greatest non-sectarian movements for peace that the world has ever known. Their biggest handicap, that prevents them from being even greater, is a shortage of leaders. Here in Derbyshire there are not just a few hundreds, but several thousand girls who can't be Guides simply for a lack of leaders.

When BP took those boys to Brownsea Island in 1907, he could never have envisaged that this would be the start of an organization that has lasted over one hundred years. Brownsea Island, set in Poole Harbour, Dorset, has now become known as the birthplace of Scouting.

The island was privately owned until acquired by the National Trust in 1962, and at their invitation, Lady Baden-Powell officially opened Brownsea Island in 1963. It has been described as an atmospheric, 500 acre island of health and woodland, but the island is only open to visitors from April to October.

In 1967, Lady Baden-Powell unveiled a commemorative stone on Evening Hill, Poole to commemorate the borough's close association with Scouting. Also to see, inside St Mary's Church, Brownsea Island is a monument to the marriage of Lord and Lady Baden-Powell, and in 2007, the Baden-Powell Centre was opened on the island providing indoor hostel accommodation and 50 acres of camping.

But if Brownsea Island is the birthplace of Scouting, Crystal Palace Park must be the birthplace of Guiding. It was here at the first big Scout Rally held on September 4th 1909 that the girls turned up and demanded to be included. It is therefore very significant that on Saturday September 5th 2009, to mark the launch of Guiding's Centenary Celebrations, the historic maze in Crystal Palace Park which has been completely renovated and redesigned by the organization, was officially opened by Girlguiding UK.

THE CHESTERFIELD TRAIL

5·25km – (3¼ miles)

We hope that visitors from many parts will be attracted to Chesterfield to see Olave's roots and for this reason, this walk has been devised to help you discover and appreciate Chesterfield's guiding connections and the old Chesterfield that Olave would have known.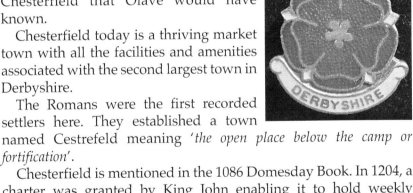

Chesterfield today is a thriving market town with all the facilities and amenities associated with the second largest town in Derbyshire.

The Romans were the first recorded settlers here. They established a town named Cestrefeld meaning *'the open place below the camp or fortification'*.

Chesterfield is mentioned in the 1086 Domesday Book. In 1204, a charter was granted by King John enabling it to hold weekly markets, now on Monday, Friday and Saturday with a popular flea market on Thursdays. Over the years the town has developed around the Market Place. In 1723, Daniel Defoe, on his travels through Chesterfield described the town as *'a handsome populous town, well built and well inhabited with a very good market well-stored with provisions'*.

The same observation could be made of our present day town. Guides are encouraged to be observant and on this walk we point

119

out landmarks and prominent buildings, giving a short history to make your walk more enjoyable. In the worst scenario, by taking notice of the landmarks going, you should always be able to turn round and find your way back again.

For added fun the instructions include compass directions. If you think of north as the top, south is opposite at the bottom. WE is seperated to west on the left and east on the right. Another way of remembering is to recite – Never Eat Shredded Wheat – the initials trace round in a clockwise direction.

When you start on this walk, take note of what direction you are going. The sun rises in the east, so at six o'clock in the morning the sun is due east. At nine o'clock the sun is south-east, (midway between south and east) and at midday it is due south. At three in the afternoon it is south-west, and at six o'clock it is due west.

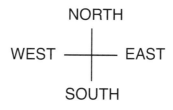

NORTH

WEST ———|——— EAST

SOUTH

LAY A PIN ACROSS THE
FACE TO INDICATE
NORTH/SOUTH. THE PIN
POINTS NORTH

USE YOUR WATCH TO TELL DIRECTION
Not everyone has a compass but most people possess a watch which can be used to tell direction – not a digital variety. Line the watch up with the hour hand pointing towards the sun. Take a blade of grass, a pin or something similar to use as a pointer and place this across the watch face passing straight over the centre point. Line this pointer up midway between the hour hand and the 12. This is your north/south direction.

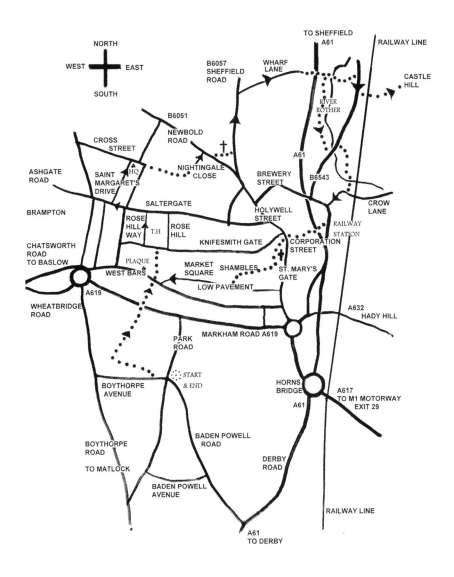

THE WALK

We begin our walk at the junction of Baden-Powell Road and Park Road. SK381:707.

Baden-Powell Road links the main A61 Derby Road at SK383;701 to Park Road at SK381;707, as it leads towards the town. Off Baden-Powell Road is Baden-Powell Avenue.

From the mid 1800's onwards, Mayors and Aldermen, Prime Ministers and War Heroes gave their names to the streets of Chesterfield, although many who once enjoyed the admiration of the nation are now almost completely forgotten. We have Gladstone Road (named after the prime minister) and Stephenson's Place (railway engineer) but who today would know that Redvers Buller Road celebrates the military career of Redvers Henry Buller (1839-1908) who fought the Chinese, the Ashanti, the Kaffirs and the Zulus, gained the Victoria Cross and became Commander in Chief of British forces in the Second Boer War?

Another distinguished war general and hero of the Boer War was Baden-Powell, but while ever there are Scouts and Guides, his name will never be forgotten.

Park Road which borders the eastern edge of Queens Park originally ran straight into the Market Place but has now been cut by Markham Road and New Beetwell Street.

From the junction with Baden-Powell Road, look north down Park Road towards the town. At the end of the houses on your right, the Lancashire, Derbyshire & East Coast Railway line used to pass over Park Road on a high embankment as it ran from the terminus at the Market Place opposite West House to Horns Bridge SK387;707. The embankment was demolished in the 1950's.

❏   Turn west. Cross Park Road and go almost straight ahead into Boythorpe Avenue. This road runs between Queen's Park and Queen's Park Annex.

❑ At the entrance gates to the park on your right, enter Queen's Park which was formerly part of the Maynard estate know as Maynard's Meadow. Follow the path west walking almost parallel to Boythorpe Avenue to reach the Bandstand, an obvious eye-catcher in the park. The band stand is a tribute to the efforts of Alderman Wood who instigated the idea to make a park to celebrate Queen Victoria's Golden Jubilee in 1887. The park includes twenty two acres complete with boating lake, and from the very beginning it was used for a wealth of sporting and cultural activities including the first county cricket match which was played here in June 1898 when Derbyshire entertained Surrey. Over on the outskirts of the park to your west is the Queen's Park Sport's Centre which was opened in 1987. Activities here include swimming and comprehensive keep-fit and fitness programmes.

THE BAND STAND WITH THE MARKET HALL ON THE SKY LINE TO THE LEFT

❑ Facing north towards the town with the Crooked Spire on the horizon on your right, the Market Hall midway, and the Town Hall on the left, head towards the iron footbridge over Markham Road. Markham Road ran along the track bed of the Midland Railway, Brampton Branch.

From the vantage point of the bridge, turn and look over to the west. This is Brampton and just behind the roundabout in the distance is the site of Brampton Brewery SK375;711.

The Brampton area was famous for its

THE ORIGINAL BRAMPTON BREWERY LOGO DEPICTING A WELL MUSCLED ARM HOLDING UP A BRICK HAMMER IMPLIES HEALTH AND STRENGTH industries; the brewery, the brick works, the factories, foundries and potteries. The local potters produced a pottery named Brampton Ware, an unglazed earthenware which is now much sought after by collectors.

Brampton Brewery can be traced back to 1839 when along with the factories and the potteries, the brewery was a cornerstone of the local community. It was purchased by the Soames family in 1877 and remained in their possession until June 1897. In 1902, the brewery was partly destroyed by fire. The new build on an adjacent site became the first electrically driven brewery in the country. The next fifty years saw various changes not always for the better and in June 1955, the last Brampton Brew was produced and the brewery was closed. The building was taken over by various light industries until it was demolished in 1984 when a superstore was built on the site.

But that's not the end of the story. After an absence of over 50 years, Brampton Brewery was reborn in the winter of 2007. A small team of local enthusiasts, led by head brewer Chris Radford, re-established Brampton Brewery at the former East Midland Electricity Board site on Chatsworth Road. This was formerly the Chesterfield Corporation Tramway Depot at 172 Chatsworth Road, constructed in 1904 at the start of the electric tramway operations. It's just 200 yards away from the birth place of the original brewery. The first brew made by the new brewery was *Golden Bud*, named after a brand brewed at the original Brampton Brewery.

❏　　　Leave the vantage point of the bridge and walk north between the buildings of the PCC and Post Office Counters to a

pedestrian crossing. This is West Bars and ahead is the Town Hall. The name West Bars denotes the barriers that once stood here to prevent cattle straying into town.

❏　　　Cross West Bars and continue to walk north into what were the grounds of West House, now known as

WEST HOUSE FORMERLY STOOD ON THIS SITE

Shentall's gardens. Branch west towards the individual office building built in the 1970's as the Chesterfield Court House. Here you will find the Blue Plaque dedicated to Olave, Lady Baden-Powell. SK378;712 unveiled on February 22nd 2011. www.derbyshire.gov.uk/blueplaques

❏   Return to the central path and walk north up to the cenotaph. This area is known as Rose Hill after the property that once stood here. Chesterfield Corporation bought the Rose Hill estate which extended to about nine acres to build the new town hall and Rose Hill and its neighbour West House were both demolished in 1936. The foundation stone of the Town Hall was laid on April 15th 1936 and the building was officially opened by Her Grace the Duchess of Devonshire on April 6th 1938 at a cost of £142,500.

❏   Branch west, then north as you cross the road and walk round the Town Hall into Rose Hill Way which leads to Saltergate. As the name suggests, it was probably the route used by the salt merchants from Cheshire, and it led to the earliest known market site in the town at Holywell Cross. But off Saltergate is a street named Glumangate and it's been suggested that these old names reflect the fact that carcasses of livestock were salted at Saltergate and bones finished up at Glumangate to be made into glue.

❏   Turn west and after one hundred metres, pause at the two stone statues outside the offices of the Derbyshire Miner's Association. Chesterfield has not been eager to mark a local hero's life with a statue, which makes these two figures of James Haslam and William Edwin Harvey exceptional. Haslam was born in 1842 and at the age of ten went to work in the mines where generation after generation of men had the inevitable life sentence of hard labour. Life for over 10,000 miners and their families in and around Chesterfield was then characterised by unremitting toil, poor wages and squalid living conditions.

In 1881 the established miner's union broke up and Haslam was asked to create a new organisation. With the help of William Edward Harvy who had also been born into proverty and entered the mines when aged ten, the Derbyshire Miner's Association was launched. These two highly respected, popular figures even impressed the colliery owners and local notables with their negotiating skills and quiet determination. In 1893 both Harvey and Haslam were made magistrates, an amazing achievement for men of their background, then in 1906 Haslam took the Chesterfield seat as a Labour candidate and ten months later Harvey took the North-East Derbyshire ward in a by-election. The rough accent of these two Chesterfield working men made itself heard amongst the decision makers at the capital, creating a better life for miners and working folks everywhere.

❏   Cross Saltergate and the end of Tennyson Avenue, then turn north into St Margaret's Drive. At the end at the T junction with Cross Street is the Chesterfield Guide Headquarters SK378;716, opened by Lady Baden-Powell on May 16th 1930. The Hall can be booked for private engagements on an individual or regular basis, for Guiding and non-Guiding events. A Guide volunteer shop, putting money back into local guiding is open on the premises every Tuesday evening and the first Saturday morning in the month. All enquiries 01246 278336.

Girlguiding

Chesterfield Girl Guide

Headquarters

THE
CHESTERFIELD
GUIDE
HEADQUARTERS

126

❏ Turn east and walk straight ahead. Leaving the road to walk through the cutting between the buildings. On your left is the Roman Catholic Church of the Annunciation. On reaching Spencer Street, cross to the marked passageway between the high walls and follow the path as it skirts the Derbyshire County NHS Primary Care Trust premises on your left. Continue until reaching a gate on your left signed 'pedestrian access only'. Go through into the car park and continue round the NHS Trust building to a barrier at the end of Nightingale Close. Most of this is new build, but the large old re-vamped buildings were the old Workhouse of the Chesterfield Poor Law Union, built on open fields in 1839-40.

THE OLD WORKHOUSE – LATER SCARSDALE HOSPITAL

This building held 300 paupers, men, women and children seg-regated according to sex. Later it was extended to be used by the whole community as Scarsdale Hospital.

❏ Walk north down Nightingale Close to arrive at Newbold Road. At the beginning of the 19th century, Newbold Road still lay across fields and was used mainly by drovers with sheep and cattle for the Chesterfield market and by farm people with their surplus produce to sell. The first market was established in Chesterfield 800 years ago just north of the church. As the Sheriff of Derbyshire recorded in the Pipe Rolls, it was earning a sum of £1.2s.7d for the Crown in 1165.

Across the road is Holy Trinity Church built on land donated by the Duke of Devonshire. The foundation stone was laid in 1837 and the church was consecrated in 1840. George Stephenson, the railway engineer, founder of several successful business enterprises in the area and local benefactor is buried in the chancel. His son Robert Stephenson was P.B's godfather. He was buried in

HOLY TRINITY CHURCH

Westminster Abbey. The principle memorial to George Stephenson is the church's magnificent east window depicting his home at Tapton, his works at Clay Cross and the façade of the North Midland Railway's Chesterfield station.

❏ Cross Newbold Road and continuing north/north east cut through the graveyard stretching between Newbold Road and Sheffield Road which used to be the main route out of Chesterfield to the north.

❏ Turn north, then cross the road to go east down Wharf Lane. This area would have been crammed with Victorian Warehouses

serving the Chesterfield Canal which transported coal, lead, iron, stone, corn, lime and timber to the river at Bawtry and then to Hull. The canal was a successful artery of trade for Derbyshire for 100 years, carrying a considerable traffic until the coming of the railways in the 1840s - 50s took over its trade.

HERE THE RIVER ROTHER MERGES WITH THE CHESTERFIELD CANAL

❏ Walk to the end of Wharf Lane to reach a foot bridge over the

A61 which was the former tack bed of the Great Central Railway. The placing of this line was the final nail in the canal's coffin as the railway line segregated the wharf from the canal. By 1905, the era of canal transportation had come to an end and the canal became an eye-sore. Most of the canal in Derbyshire was sold off but after a £3 million restoration project was put into operation in July 2002 one section was fully restored and open for navigation with trips available on the Chesterfield Canal Trust's passenger boat, the John Varley. At the time of writing, this area is undergoing a major redevelopment scheme, that may affect the pathways, so 'be prepared'.

❏　　　Leave the bridge and continue on the path east, crossing the River Rother which just beyond this point merges with the canal.

❏　　　Head east for the steps beside the buildings up onto the main B6543, Brimington Road.

❏　　　Cross the road, veering right to a bridge over the railway line. This is Tapton Park and if you go north/northeast to follow the drive up the hill you will arrive at Tapton House, the former home of George Stephenson whose son Robert was BP's god-father. When the Romans arrived here, they gave the town the Roman name 'Cestrefeld' meaning 'the open field near the camp'. The camp in the form of a fortified castle was set on this hill, thus the name Castle Hill.

❏　　　To resume our walk it's necessary to retrace our steps west, back to Brimington Road and the footpath that goes south beside the river to Holbeck Close and the B6543.

❏　　　Cross the road and veer east, taking the road opposite – Tapton Terrace which then goes south. Follow this track until meeting Crow Lane beside the traffic lights. Turn west and as Crow Lane opens out, the Midland Railway is on your left. At the doorway is an impressive bronze statue of George Stephenson and inside the reception hall is a blue-plaque. George Stephenson was nominated to receive this award at the same time as Olave.

❏　　　Leave the station and walk west/southwest towards the town, passing on the left of the Chesterfield Hotel, previously the Station Hotel. Cross on the pedestrian footbridge over the A61 and continue west up Corporation Street which prior to the building of the inner relief road was the main road to the station.

On your left is the Pomegranate Theatre. It used to be the Civic Theatre but had a name change in January 1982 This rather unusual name is derived from the motif of the Pomegranate tree that was introduced to the Borough seal in 1598. Catherine of Aragon, Henry VIII's first wife is said to have brought the pomegranate into Britain, although why it was chosen for the Chesterfield seal is a mystery. The seal is no longer used, but the Pomegranate can still be seen on the Borough Coat of Arms and the Chesterfield Guide Standard.

THE BOROUGH COAT OF ARMS

The pomegranate tree which in heraldic terms is 'eradicated' – torn up from the roots and 'fructed' – bearing fruit, is supported by the figures of a Cock and Pynot (local word for magpie). They both wear ducal crowns, a reference to the Duke of Devonshire's part in what has become known as the Glorious Revolution of 1688 which was plotted in an old Chesterfield ale house called The Cock and Pynot. The central figure on top of the crest is the Derby Ram while the motto refers in punning fashion to Chesterfield's crooked spire.

This whole building is the Stephenson Memorial Hall built in George's honour through public subscription, and at the end is the museum which opened its doors in May 1994. Prior to this it was the library, but that is now housed in the pavements shopping centre.

We are at the junction of St Mary's Gate and Holywell Cross, just two examples of Chesterfield streets that bear old names and carry a little bit of local history. St Mary's Gate is a clear indication of a main highway with a gate that blocked the south entrance to the town. Holywell, reminds us that here was a Holy Well, the resort of pious pilgrims or those looking for a miracle cure.

❑   Cross to the Parish Church of St Mary and All Saints with its crooked spire which is one of the architectural curiosities of this age. It is 228ft high, octagonal in plan and slopes with an eye arresting twist that can be seen from most approaches into the town.

More commonly known as the Crooked Spire, this is one of the most interesting churches in Derbyshire, built between 1210-1377 on the site of at least two previous structures. The remarkable spire was added during the fourteenth century, but as it reached two hundred feet high, the green timbers began to twist under the heavy, herringbone pattern of the lead slates. By the finished height of two hundred and twenty eight feet,

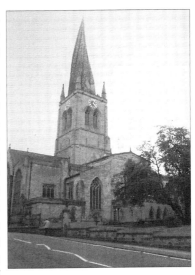

THE CROOKED SPIRE

the tilt and bulge leaned over 8'6" (2.632m) to the south and 3'9" (1.53m) to the west.

Superstition and legend surround this unusual shape, the most widely known relates to the involvement of the Devil. Apparently on his way between Derby and Sheffield, the Devil paused for a rest on the top of the spire and wound his scaly tale round it to prevent his Satanic majesty falling off. While there, a wedding was taking place in the church and anxious to see the bridal couple as they left, he leaned forward. He was so surprised to see that the bride was a virgin, he leaned a little too far to get a better look and in so doing, twisted the spire. There is also a sequel to the tale. The locals joke that the spire will straighten if ever a virgin gets married in the church. A tall story!

❏   Go south through the churchyard to Rykneld Square. The modern building ahead is the Information Centre. The name Rykneld comes from the Roman Road that passed through the area.

❏   Leaving Rykneld Square walk west down Burlington Street until this is crossed by Packers Row. This is probably a corruption of Pack Horse Row as it was once the main highway and trading route through the town. It could have been where the pack horses were loaded or unloaded.

When the Gas and Water Company shut off the gas supply to Chesterfield's street lamps in 1881, the corporation gave electric lighting a three week trial. Chesterfield therefore can make the claim of being the first town in England to have electric street lighting, but when the suppliers wanted to run further wires for the more profitable lighting of shops and homes, the corporation withdrew their support. The Gas and Water Company returned with more favourable terms and Chesterfield reverted to gaslight in 1884.

We are now on the northeastern edge of an area called The Shambles. For centuries the narrow alleyways that made up the town continued all the way from the bounds of the Parish Church to the Shambles which along with the market place were laid out and developed as long ago as the 13th century.

❏   Turn south down Packers Row, then almost immediately west to walk through the centre of the Shambles in an east/west direction.

THE CLOTHING HALL AT THE BOTTOM OF PACKERS ROW WITH THE FIRST GAS LAMP IN CHESTERFIELD c1890

It is thought that the present street layout in the Shambles here closely resembles the lines of the alleys between the mediaeval market stalls, and the name comes from the time when animals were butchered here. This area has changed dramatically since the days when a bye-law existed that any animals brought into town for slaughter had to be baited in the belief that this tenderised the meat.

❏   Pause at the Royal Oak which stands on the corner of Iron Gate in the very centre of The Shambles. According to a plaque outside, it was built in the 12th century, is the oldest inn in Chesterfield, and one of the oldest in England. That is not strictly accurate. It may be one of the oldest buildings, but it was originally a small dwelling house and did not become licensed as an inn until 1772 when it was extended into two adjacent buildings to provide stabling and a brew house. A further extension of the property took place in the mid-19th century when two butchers shops were added onto the licensed premises of George & William Batteson, maltsters.

❏ Continue through The Shambles to arrive at the Market Place. The market was moved here from the site by the church some time during the 1220's. On the northern side of the Market Place

THE SHAMBLES WITH THE ROYAL OAK ON THE RIGHT

was the Angel Hotel where the auction for the sale of Brampton Brewery took place in May 1877. It closed in 1915, but after a disastrous fire in 1917 which destroyed most of the building, it was totally demolished in 1926. The site was purchased by the Westminster Bank.

Due west of you is the Market Hall, built in 1857 on the site of an earlier building that was also used for purposes connected with the market. The clock was presented to the town by the Duke of Devonshire in 1867. It's an impressive building, but not to everyone's taste; Nicolas Pevsner described it as 'the crudest show of High Victorian provincial prosperity'.

❏ Walk west towards the market hall and locate the Market Place water pump. Back in the 17th and 18th centuries, the people of Chesterfield drew their water from the Rivers Hipper and Rother for everyday use, but for drinking they relied upon springs and wells (and Brampton Brewery). This Market pump which was rebuilt in 1825 drew its supply of drinkable water from deep underground, but like many wells and springs, in dry weather it was not reliable and the supply would cease. In 1825 provision was made to supply piped water which was stored in a 75ft diameter reservoir on West Street. It was untreated which meant that it was cloudy and had a rather unpleasant smell. It was said that it was so murky, the poor used it as soup, the middle classes used it only for washing their clothes and the elite for watering their gardens.

❏ Turn south to reach Low Pavement that runs along the south side of the Market Place. Most of this was included in the Town Centre Development and is now part of the Pavements Shopping Centre.

Between MacDonald's and Boots the chemist was the upper section of Tontine road. Now it's just a pedestrian walk way to the shopping centre and the library. Before they were all destroyed the buildings in this area between Low Pavement and the River Hipper were known as the Dog Kennels. They became overcrowded and unsanitary and many were demolished between 1912-1914 when Markham Road and Tontine Road were built. The remainder which were behind the frontages of Low Pavement were demolished in 1979, but the front facades were retained. The project was completed in October 1981 at a cost of £12,000,000 and has gained many awards.

❏ Walk west along Low Pavement with the Market Hall on your right until reaching The Peacock located near the far end of Low Pavement. This was the former information centre housed in a 16th century wooden framed building which was thought to have been a medieval Guild Hall, but more recently a public house. The building was restored in 1981 and is now a tea room.

You are now at an area called New Square which was added to the market area in 1829. It was known as Swine's Green until the end of the 18th century, and was nothing more than a marshy patch of land much loved by local pigs for common grazing and later formed part of the market area where the sheep and pigs were sold. Below the Market Place was Toll Nook where livestock would be penned either before or after the herders paid the fee for entering through the west bars. Before the opening of the new cattle market in 1900, Swine's Green was the regular herding place for livestock awaiting sale or slaughter. The scene must have resembled a large farmyard with horses, cattle, sheep, pigs, drovers and farmers thronging every street around the Market Place.

Continue west along Low Pavement leaving New Square, and between the shops on your right is The Sun Inn. The original 17th century inn on the site was a busy coaching inn and although this building dates from around 1920 the basement and cellars are part of that original 17th century inn. This was one of the inns owned by Brampton Brewery and etched on the window is the brewery's Health, Strength Logo.

Across the road is the Portland Hotel, so there was obviously quite a lot of competition between these two establishments and Park Hotel & Restaurant all within a very small area. The Market Place station of the LD&EC Railway was next door to the Portland Hotel, directly opposite the Sun Inn.

You are now back at the site of West House and grounds where the blue plaque to Lady Baden-Powell is displayed.

Cross the road and retrace your steps south, over Markham Road into Queen's Park, and out onto Boythorpe Avenue. Turn east to reach Baden Powell Road which is the start/end of this walk.

THE OLD SUN INN, WEST BARS

DERBYSHIRE PLACES
MENTIONED IN THIS BOOK

To make your visit enjoyable and memorable why not explore some of the other places mentioned in this book and discover Derbyshire? Chesterfield makes a great base for exploring the surrounding towns and villages that are steeped in history and tradition. They are well worth a visit, and details can be obtained from the Chesterfield Tourist Information Centre, Rykneld Square, Chesterfield – next to the Crooked Spire.

GLENBROOK RESIDENTIAL CENTRE

There are places to stay to suit every taste and pocket, but Derbyshire is also fortunate to have Glenbrook, a Girlguide Residential Centre situated in the delightful Derbyshire Peak District.

Glenbrook was opened in 1968 by Olave Lady Baden Powell. After her death, the family received thousands of tributes and individual letters from people who had met her, even briefly but had been impressed by this amazing woman. This is one such letter sent to The Hon. Mrs Betty Clay, Lady Baden Powell's daughter, and Mr Robin Clay has kindly allowed it to be used in this book.

'I was at the Glenbrook opening when Lady Baden-Powell came along through the guard of honour. She turned her head, recognised the lady next to me and came over. Saying 'Hello', she addressed her by name and shook her hand saying how lovely it was to see her again.

After she had gone on, the lady next to me gasped and said, 'I don't believe it!' She then went on to tell me that she had met Lady

Baden-Powell ten years earlier and then only briefly. It was aston-
ishing that she had remembered her name after all this time, amid
all the hundreds of people worldwide that she had met meanwhile.'

Glenbrook is in the scenic Hope Valley seventeen miles from
Chesterfield and offers three camping fields, accommodating 100
campers in six designated camping areas.

Contact warden@glenbrook79.freeserve.co.uk. Telephone 01509
552658

STUBBING COURT, WINGERWORTH

Although extended considerably by several housing developments, Wingerworth still remains rural in character.

According to the 1086 Domesday Book, Wingerworth was then
called Wingreurde meaning Wingre's enclosure. All Saints Church,
Wingerworth SK383;674 dates from this late Anglo-Saxon, early
Norman period, with a considerable extension in 1964.

The manor of Wingerworth was given to the Brailsford family in
the 12th century, later to the Curzons of Kedleston and in the 16th
century it came into the possession of the Hunlokes. Thomas
Windsor Hunloke built a handsome Georgian mansion on the site
of at least two earlier manor houses, but the family fortunes
fluctuated over the years. In 1801 the population of Wingerworth
was 500, 100 years later it had fallen to 349.

In May 1920, Wingerworth Hall and 260 acres were offered for
sale. There were no takers so the land was sold off piecemeal and
the Hall demolished. All that now remains are the north and south
blocks, the stable block and several gate houses – all private residences.

At this sale, Mr Burkett the owner of Stubbing Court purchased
the Great Pond SK362;673 and a considerable area of wood and
farm land which lies on the eastern edge of the Stubbing Court
estate. It is now known as Stubbing Pond.

Stubbing Court was Olave's birthplace and as it is still privately
owned any intrusion on the privacy of the owners would not be
welcome. The last time it was sold was in 1953 when the then
owner G.C.M. Jackson was leaving the district. He gave instructions to Henry Spencer and Sons estate agents, and on June 25th

1953 the estate consisting of 415 acres of parkland, farmland and gardens was bought by John Adlington, a local builder who developed much of Wingerworth. Now owned by his descendents, part of Stubbing Court is Stubbing Court Riding offering equine master classes, and part is a private Dental Practice.

The best way to see the house is to take a walk round Stubbing Pond. There is a footpath from Watson Lane just above the boat house, that goes along the hillside above Stubbing Pond. Continue on the path until meeting a junction of paths, then turn left. This will bring you to Malthouse Lane. Turn left and follow the road which runs along the front boundary wall of Stubbing Court SK357;672. Cross the rather quaint bridge to return to Watson Lane.

RENISHAW HALL SK438;786

Renishaw Hall is the Derbyshire home of the Sitwell family. It is situated on the edge of the village of Eckington, seven miles from Chesterfield. It is still very much a family home which adds to its unique atmosphere.

Special group tours and public tours (Friday only and bookable in advance) of the hall are new for 2011. This will enable you to see some of the spectacular collections of art and furniture that have been acquired by generations of Sitwells. It is quite literally a treasure trove.

You can also take a tour with the head gardener and there are special events throughout the season. In May 1994, a museum and Arts Centre was opened in the beautiful Georgian stable block, summer opening only, and Renishaw also can boast of some excellent wines made from grapes grown in their own vineyard at one time the most northerly in Europe.

For tours call: 01246 43231: enquiries@renishaw-hall.co.uk

THE CRICH TRAMWAY VILLAGE SK346;548

The first horse drawn tramcars in Chesterfield began on November 8th 1882, and ran from Brampton to Chesterfield Market Hall along West Bars. The service started operating with three vehicles, two being double deck and one single. In 1890 a further two single deck trams were added.

In 1904, the Bill for a new electric tramway passed through Parliament and the new service came into operation on December 21st 1904, running from Brampton to Whittington Moor. After the First World War, the popularity of the tramway system went into decline. This was partly due to the high cost of repairing vehicles and track, and the last tram ran on May 23rd 1927. The service continued with trolley buses.

One of the earliest horse-drawn trams that ran along West Bars was No.8. It was saved and after extensive restoration in 1982, placed on loan to the National Tramway Museum at Crich, Derbyshire.

Opened in 1959, the Tramway Museum Society are constantly adding relics from the past to show this early form of transport, but they are not just preserving the trams in a museum. The site at Crich was originally a quarry complete with railway and when the National Tramway Museum took over the disused site they reinstated the railway so that future generations of visitors are not only able to see the trams but can take a ride in them too.

Crich is off the A6 Matlock to Derby road, twelve miles from Chesterfield. The museum is open April-October. 01773 854321.

CHATSWORTH HOUSE SK260702

Chatsworth House is one of England's best loved houses, in a splendid setting on the banks of the River Derwent at Baslow, ten miles west of Chesterfield. The house contains one of the best collections of paintings, furniture, tapestries, china, sculpture and plate, collected by fifteen generations of Cavendishes. The 105 acre garden is famous for its landscape, fountains and cascade. The Park is about 1,100 acres surrounded by a deer fence nine miles long, and over the years there have been numerous Guiding and Scouting events held in this park including the Guide Jubilee in 1960.

There is also a farmyard and adventure playground, estate shops, restaurant and tea rooms. Special events take place in the Park during the season including the Angling Fair in May and the Horse Trails in October. The house is seasonal opening but the grounds are open all year round.

DERBYSHIRE COUNTY COUNCIL

LADY
BADEN-POWELL
1889 - 1977
World Chief Guide

Lived as a girl at West House
in these grounds